Butter My Butt and Call Me a Biscuit

You're the Butter on My Biscuit!

Butter My Butt and Call Me a Biscuit

AND

You're the Butter on My Biscuit!

And Other Country Sayings, Say-Sos, Hoots, and Hollers

Allan Zullo and Gene Cheek

Andrews McMeel
PUBLISHING®

Butter My Butt and Call Me a Biscuit
And
You're the Butter on My Biscuit!:
And Other Country Sayings, Say-Sos, Hoots, and Hollers

Andrews McMeel Publishing, LLC
an Andrews McMeel Universal company
1130 Walnut Street, Kansas City, Missouri 64106

www.andrewsmcmeel.com

19 20 21 22 23 SDB 10 9 8 7 6 5 4 3

ISBN: 978-1-4494-3017-7

The material in this book previously appeared in
Butter My Butt and Call Me a Biscuit (Andrews McMeel
Publishing, 2009) and *You're the Butter on My Biscuit!*
(Andrews McMeel Publishing, 2010).

ATTENTION: SCHOOLS AND BUSINESSES
Andrews McMeel books are available at quantity
discounts with bulk purchase for educational, business,
or sales promotional use. For information,
please e-mail the Andrews McMeel Publishing
Special Sales Department: specialsales@amuniversal.com

To the good people of my adopted
community of Fairview, North Carolina.
—A.Z.

To my friends and family for
putting up with me all these years.
—G.C.

Contents

Gooder 'n Grits

The sayings, saws, and slogans from country folk—the down-home people of the farms, mountains, and ranges of America—are corny, clever, and colorful. There's almost always an element of truth in these beliefs from the backwoods and front porches, reflecting a way of thinking that can touch us all in different ways.

Conjured up during an era when our country was country, they have endured over time and offer us, in our frazzled techno-crazed 24/7 media-frenzied world, an opportunity to laugh and to ponder. As Maya Angelou once said, "Listen carefully to what country people call mother wit. In those homely sayings are couched the collective wisdom of generations."

We have collected hundreds of endearing, truthful, and amusing homespun adages and turns of phrases, and dozens of countrified jokes that we think will appeal to anyone who wants a change of pace in our pop culture–infused life.

Living in North Carolina's Blue Ridge Mountains for years—Gene is a born-and-bred Tar Heel—we and our families have learned to appreciate the way country folk paint their sentences in the most vivid and original analogies, sew simple words together into tapestries of truisms, and pepper their language with zesty wit. We've heard their sayings and 'laughed at jokes sprung from strange-sounding hollows, hamlets, and hinterlands. Real places like Possum Trot, Rabbit Hop, Pumpkintown, Tobaccoville, Licklog, Hardscrabble, Sodom, Climax, Matrimony, Trust, Tick Bite, Lizard Lick, Toast, Fig, Snapfinger, Bucksnort, Goose Hollow, and Bear Wallow.

It's not just in North Carolina that you can find expressive phrases, metaphors, and axioms. You can hear them in the accented voices of folks from Appalachia to the Adirondacks, from the cornfields of Illinois to the rangelands of Texas, from the forests of the great Northwest to the deserts of the sprawling Southwest. Country sayings are as varied as America itself and part of our national heritage. Best of all, they're just fun to read as all get out.

We hope that for you, reading this collection of country sayings and jokes is gooder 'n tupelo honey over hot grits.

—Allan Zullo and Gene Cheek

NEVER KICK A COW PATTY ON A HOT DAY

(And Other Pearls of Wisdom)

Consequences

Don't let your mouth write checks
that your rear end can't cash.

Inaction

You'll sit a long time with your
mouth wide open before a roasted
chicken flies in.

Putting on Airs

Even if you are in high cotton,
don't get above your raisin'.

Wishful Thinking

Wish in one hand, spit in the other,
and see which one gets full faster.

Excuses

Excuses are like backsides—
everybody's got one.

Revenge

Two wrongs don't make a right,
but they sure do make it even.

Owning Up

The easiest way to eat crow is
while it's still warm, 'cause
the colder it gets, the harder
it is to swallow.

Facing Reality

You can put your boots
in the oven, but that don't
make 'em biscuits.

A Light at the End of the Tunnel

The country doctor arrives at a cabin with no electricity in a hollow so deep they have to pipe in the sunshine. Inside are Fester and his wife, Tweetie, who's about to squeeze out their first baby.

During the delivery, the doc asks Fester to hold the lantern close to Tweetie so he can see. Soon, out pops the infant. Fester starts to put the lantern down when the doc hollers, "Wait a minute, hold that lantern back up here, Fester. There's another baby a-comin'!" Sure enough, Tweetie delivers a second infant.

Fester goes to place the lantern on the table when the good doctor yells out, "Well, pick my peas! Here comes another one!"

Fester is swooning from the news. "Doc," he says, "you reckon it's the light that's attractin' 'em?"

Lies

If you pile up too many lies, the ground will be so steep you'll skin your nose climbin' up 'em.

Unnecessary Risks

Don't hit a hornets' nest with a short stick.

Compliments

Sayin' somethin' nice makes the old feel young and the poor feel rich.

Deceit

Twistin' the truth is like puttin' perfume on a pig.

Restraint

If you're outnumbered, best keep your mouth shut, or they'll tear your butt up like a tater field that's just been plowed.

Adversity

What doesn't kill you makes
you stronger.

Seeking Advice

Never ask a barber if he thinks
you need a haircut.

Self-Help

If you want help,
look to the end of your arm.

Imperfection

Every dog ought to have
a few fleas.

Knowing Whom
to Criticize

Never smack a man
chewin' tobacco.

Investing

The quickest way to double your
money is to fold it over and put it
back in your pocket.

Talking Dirty

A high-society lady was mortified when her daughter came home from college engaged to a young man with little money and no social standing. The dreaded day came when the haughty woman had to introduce her soon-to-be son-in-law to her friends. She winced as the young man talked to the snooty matrons in language that was neither grammatical nor refined. She couldn't have been more embarrassed if she had mistakenly served her guests moonshine instead of sweet tea.

The eyebrows of the hoity-toity were arched so high you could drive a team of horses through them. Rather than swoon in shame, the lady gritted her teeth and said to her daughter, who was still gazing starry-eyed at the ne'er-do-well, "Darlin', why don't you and your young man slip out to the kitchen and bring us some more cake?"

As the door closed behind them, Mrs. High-and-Mighty lowered her voice to her friends and said, "Well, you know, even the most fertile lands must be manured from time to time."

Inaction

You'll never plow the field by
turnin' it over in your mind.

Guilt

It's always the dirty dog
that howls the loudest.

Knowledge

Live and learn
or die and know it all.

Excuses

Excuses are like armpits —
everyone has got at least two,
and they both stink.

The Company
You Keep

If you lie down with dogs,
you get up with fleas.

Ill-Gotten Gains

Honey is sweet, but don't
lick it off the briar.

Fake Compliments

Be careful you don't get
too sugary, or you'll drown
in your own sweet tea.

Advice

Don't give cherries to pigs
or advice to fools.

Wrong Impression

You can't tell the size of the turnips
by lookin' at their tops.

Anxiety

Worryin' gives small things
big shadows.

Opportunity

When life gives you scraps,
make a quilt.

Unwanted Relatives

Every garden has some weeds.

Promised Land

A Yankee decides to visit the grandest cathedral in each state. The first church he goes to is in California. Near the altar, he spots a golden telephone on a wall. Above it a sign reads, "$10,000 A MINUTE." The minister explains it's a direct line to heaven, so anyone who calls it can talk straight to God.

The Yankee visits cathedrals throughout the West, Midwest, and Northeast. Each time, he notices the same golden phone with the same sign. Each pastor, reverend, or priest tells him the same thing: It's a direct line to heaven.

On his first day below the Mason-Dixon Line, he enters a cathedral where, once again, he spots a golden telephone. But this time the sign reads, "25 CENTS PER CALL." He tells the pastor, "In every cathedral I've visited throughout this country, a call to God costs $10,000 a minute. How come a direct line to heaven from your golden phone costs only 25 cents?"

The pastor smiles and says, "That's easy. You're in the South now, so it's a local call."

Accountability

Don't blame the cow
when the milk goes sour.

Average Joe

We can't all be big shots.
Someone has to sit on the curb
and wave at 'em as they go by.

Unworkable Situation

There are times when the
big dog won't hunt.

Unintended Consequences

Everyone loves the deer
'til it eats from the garden.

Ego

Some people are so full
of themselves, you'd like to
buy 'em for what they're worth
and sell 'em for what they
think they're worth.

Telling Tales
out of School

At Sunday dinner, Grandma Melba asked her grandson Buster what he learned in Sunday school that morning. He eagerly told the biblical story of how Moses led the Israelites to safety from the pursuing soldiers of the Pharaoh's army. Buster said that Moses used a golden megaphone to warn all the Israelites to flee Egypt. Then, according to the lad, "Moses hired engineers and real fast workers to build a bridge over the Red Sea. Once all the Israelites crossed over safely, Moses blew up the bridge, killin' all the Egyptian soldiers who were followin' 'em."

Grandma Melba nearly fell out of her rocker after hearing the tall tale. She leaned over and asked the boy, "Is that how your teacher told the story?"

"Not exactly," Buster replied, "but you'd never believe me if I told it her way."

Impossible Task

You can't make chicken salad
out of chicken feathers.

State of Mind

A good attitude is like kudzu —
it spreads.

Bar Fight

Pickin' a bar fight is like goin'
bear huntin' with a switch.

Wrong Assumption

Just 'cause a chicken has wings
don't mean it can fly.

Liars

Figures don't lie,
but liars figure.

Needless Worry

Most problems ain't no bigger
than the little end of nothin'
whittled down to a fine point.

Ego

Every crow thinks
he's the blackest.

Optimism

There's a new day tomorrow,
and it ain't been touched yet.

Facing Reality

If your cat had kittens in
the doghouse, would that
make 'em puppies?

First Impression

You can't tell much 'bout
a chicken potpie 'til you
cut through the crust.

Exaggeration

Don't let your mouth
overload your butt.

Criticism

Never insult an alligator
'til you've crossed the creek.

Family Problems

Every man needs to skin
his own skunk.

Making Matters Worse

When bugs throw a party,
they don't invite the chickens.

Sooner
Better Than Later

Great-granddaddy Floyd turned one hundred the other day, and all his kin gathered to toss him a mighty fine shindig. Floyd, who was all spiffed up, was still sharp as a tack and had all his acorns and all his teeth.

One of his great grandsons—the first to graduate from college—asked him, "Granddaddy, if you had to live your life over, would you make the same mistakes again?"

Taking a deep drag off his corncob pipe, Floyd replied, "I surely would, only I'd start a whole lot sooner."

SOMETIMES YOU GET AND SOMETIMES YOU GET GOT

(And Other Say-Sos 'bout Good Times and Bad)

Feeling Good

I feel finer than a frog's hair split
four ways and sanded twice.

*If you're in a really good mood,
you might say . . .*

If I felt any better, I'd be
two people.

Problems

I got more problems than
I can say grace over.

*If your friend has a problem that she's
trying to ignore, you might say . . .*

If you got a rooster, he's goin'
to crow.

Blessed

I'm so blessed, I could step
in manure and come out
smellin' like a rose.

*If you're referring to a friend who came
into wealth, you might say . . .*

Now, there goes a man who
broke out in money.

Ain't No Accidents

A wet-behind-the-ears insurance agent drives out to the farm of old man Grover, hoping to get him to renew his health policy. The young fellow finds Grover tuning up his tractor, but the farmer stops what he's doing to answer a few questions.

"Have you had any accidents in the past year?" the agent asks.

"Nope," Grover replies, "although that mule over yonder kicked in two of my ribs a while back, and last spring a rattlesnake bit my ankle."

"That's terrible," says the new agent. "Wouldn't you call those accidents?"

"Naw," the farmer replies. "I pretty much thought they did it on purpose."

Hard Times

I've fallen on stony ground.

If you want to offer hope to someone who's down in the dumps, you might say . . .

We've all seen sicker dogs that got well.

Wealth

He's so rich, he buys a new boat every time his old one gets wet.

If you're well off, you might want to boast . . .

I'm richer than clabbered cream.

Poverty

I'm too poor to paint and
too proud to whitewash.

*If you're always broke,
you might say . . .*

Money thinks I'm dead.

Luck

Even a blind squirrel finds
an acorn now and then.

*If you're talking about the luck of
the Irish, you might say . . .*

He's so lucky, he could sit on a
fence and the birds would feed him.

Lip Service

Old codger Roscoe was sitting on the bench in front of the general store, whittling a gee-haw whimmy-diddle, when his friend Virgil arrived in a mule-driven wagon.

Virgil jumped off the wagon, tied the mule to a post, and then walked to the back of the animal, lifted up its tail, and planted a kiss smack dab on its rear end.

Roscoe dropped his whittling knife and said, "Did I just see what I just saw?"

Virgil nodded and said, "I reckon you did."

"Why would you do a durn fool thing like that?"

"I have a powerful bad case of chapped lips."

"And what you just did cures 'em?"

"Nope," said Virgil, "but it keeps me from lickin' 'em."

Poverty

I don't have a pot to pee in
nor a window to throw it out of.

If you're flat broke, you might say . . .

My piggy bank is as useful as an
ashtray on a motorcycle.

Good Fortune

I'm livin' on the lucky side
of the road.

*When things are going well financially,
you might say . . .*

I'm keepin' my smokehouse greasy.

Hard Times

I'm so unlucky, I wouldn't hit
water if I fell out of a boat.

*If you're talking about someone
who's a little worse for wear,
you might say . . .*

Looks like he's on the backside
of hard times.

Down in the Dumps

Oakie was madder than a wet hen as he called over his four sons and yelled, "Which one of you goldurn sprouts pushed the outhouse in the river?"

No one said a word, so Oakie calmed down and said, "Years ago, when George Washington was a boy, he cut down a cherry tree. His pa asked him, 'George, did you chop down the cherry tree?' And George told him, 'I cannot tell a lie. Yes, I did.' His pa didn't punish him 'cause he told the truth. So I ask you once again: Who pushed the outhouse in the river?"

His youngest son stepped forward and confessed, "It was me, Pa."

Oakie threw him over his knee and whaled the daylights out of him. The little boy looked at Oakie through tear-filled eyes and whined, "You said George Washington wasn't punished for confessin' he chopped down the cherry tree."

"That's true," said Oakie. "But when that happened, his pa wasn't sittin' in the tree."

Happy Days

If times get any better, I'll have to hire somebody to help me enjoy 'em.

If you're feeling extremely joyous, you might say . . .

I'm as happy as a calf in clover.

Life

One day you're drinkin' wine, the next day you're pickin' grapes.

If someone's life took a turn for the worse, you might say . . .

One day you're the peacock, the next day you're the feather duster.

Poverty

I'm so poor, I had to fry up
my nest egg.

*If you came from a poverty-stricken
childhood, you might say . . .*

We were so poor, my brother
and I had to ride double on our
stick horse.

Loyal Follower

Junior went up to his pop and announced, "Pa, I'm leavin' the hills to look for adventure, excitement, and beautiful women."

Junior went into his room and packed his meager belongings. As he turned to leave, his pop blocked the doorway, so Junior said, "Don't try to stop me, Pa. I'm on my way."

Holding up his own suitcase, his pop replied, "Who's tryin' to stop you? I'm goin' with you!"

Ups and Downs

The sun don't shine on the same
dog all the time.

*If you want to inject a little
positivism into a bleak situation,
you might say . . .*

Even a barren apple tree gives you
some shade.

Short of Cash

There's too much month left
at the end of the money.

*If you're in a bad financial situation,
you might say . . .*

I'm so broke, I'd have to borrow
money to buy a drink of water.

Taking Chances

Sometimes you're the windshield
and sometimes you're the bug.

To a gambling man, you might say . . .

Sometimes you eat the bear,
and sometimes the bear eats you.

Luck

He attracts luck like a magnet
does a horseshoe.

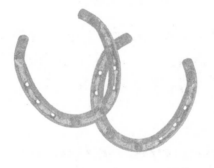

*Talking about a guy who always comes
out ahead, you might say . . .*

He can slide down a hundred-foot
locust tree with a wildcat under
each arm and never get a scratch.

Poverty

I'm so broke, I can't pay attention.

*If you're a little short of cash,
you might say . . .*

If a trip 'round the world cost
a dollar, I wouldn't make it to the
end of the driveway.

Financially Challenged

I'm as poor as gully-dirt.

*If a friend asks to borrow money
from you, and you don't have any
to lend, you might say . . .*

You went to a goat's house
lookin' for wool.

Problems

Every path has its puddles.

*If you're facing several problems
at once, you might say . . .*

I'm in a bad row of stumps.

Poverty

I'm so poor, I can't afford
tears to cry.

*If you're short on cash,
you might say . . .*

There ain't a tater in the patch.

Dilemma

I'm caught where the
wool is short.

*If you're trying to figure out which
of your problems to deal with first,
you might think . . .*

There ain't no difference
between a hornet and a yellow
jacket when they're both buzzin'
in your pants.

Bearing Down

Jethro took his wife and mother-in-law hunting way back in the hills. They spread out, looking for game. About sundown, Jethro found his wife, and the two went to collect his mother-in-law. All of a sudden, they heard the old lady screaming like a cat with its tail caught in the barn door. They rushed toward the sound, rounded a clearing, and came upon a chilling sight: the mother-in-law was backed up against a tree, face to jowls with a large, menacing bear.

"Jethro, what are we goin' to do?" wailed his wife.

"Be still," he told her. "That bear got hisself into this mess, let him get hisself out of it."

DON'T SPOIL SATURDAY NIGHT BY COUNTIN' THE TIME TO MONDAY MORNIN'

(And Other Notions 'bout Work and Play)

Great Fun

I'm havin' more fun than a
lost dog in a meat market.

*If you had a great time clogging at the
church dance, you might say . . .*

I sure tore up the pea patch.

Drinking

You're so drunk, you couldn't hit a
bull in the butt with a bass fiddle.

*If someone had too much to drink over
the weekend, you might say . . .*

You look like you've been
chasin' cars.

Chilling Out

I feel so lazy on the weekends that
I have to speed up just to stop.

*If you want to let things come as they
may, you might say . . .*

Charge it to the dust and let
the rain settle it.

Party Time

You look like you've been
sackin' wildcats and plumb
run outta sacks.

*In response to someone who asks you to
join a wild party, you might say . . .*

I'll jump on that like a duck
on a june bug.

Long Hours

I'm workin' from can to can't.

If you're going to have a long day at work, you might say . . .

It'll be dark-thirty before
I get home.

Work Experience

The new broom might
sweep clean, but the old broom
knows the corners.

*If you're touting your work experience,
you might say . . .*

The older the fiddle,
the sweeter the tune.

The Boss

He's the big cheese in this trap.

*If you're warning your co-worker
against leaving his job early without the
boss
finding out, you might say . . .*

That's like tryin' to slip sunup
past a rooster.

Bait and Switch

A Yankee was fishing off the coast of Florida when his boat capsized. He wouldn't swim to shore because he feared alligators, so he clung to the hull. When he spotted a cracker named Hump fishing off the dock, the Yankee shouted to him, "Are there any alligators in these waters?"

Hump replied, "Nope. There ain't been any in years."

The Yankee heaved a sigh of relief and, believing it was safe, he started swimming for shore. About halfway there, he asked the cracker, "How come there aren't any alligators here?"

Answered Hump, "The sharks ate 'em all."

Busy

I'm as busy as a one-legged man
at a butt-kickin' contest.

*When someone asks if you're busy,
you might say . . .*

There ain't no flies on me.

Lazy Worker

He'll never drown in his
own sweat.

*If you're referring to a nice
co-worker who is somewhat lazy,
you might say . . .*

He's a good dog, but he don't
like to hunt much.

Exhaustion

I'm so dog-tired, my butt's
draggin' out my tracks.

*If your body is telling you that you can't
work anymore, you might say . . .*

Just throw me in the chair and
call me a sack of taters.

Lazy Worker

He's always lookin' for
sundown and payday.

*If accused of being lazy,
you might say . . .*

I'm not afraid of work. I can
lay down right beside it and
go to sleep.

Difficult Work

A hard job is like forty miles
of rough road.

*When facing a difficult task,
you might say . . .*

That ain't no hill for a climber.

Overwhelmed

I'm so far over my head, I have to
look up to see bottom.

*When you're swamped with work
and can't seem to get ahead,
you might say . . .*

I feel like a rubber-nosed
woodpecker in a petrified forest.

Gone Fishin'

Two country boys are at their special fishing hole when all of a sudden, the game warden jumps out of the bushes.

One of the boys throws down his rod and hightails it through the woods like a fox on fire, but the warden is hot on his heels. About a half mile later, the boy stops and stoops over with his hands on his thighs to catch his breath.

The game warden finally collars him and says, "Let's see your fishin' license, boy."

The lad pulls out his wallet and shows the warden a valid fishing license.

"Well, son," says the warden, "you must be dumb as a box of rocks. You have a license, so you didn't have to run away from me."

"I reckon not, sir," replies the boy, "but my friend back yonder, well, he don't have one."

Management

They think they know everythin',
but they're as lost as geese
in a snowstorm.

*If you're hassled at work by
management, you might say . . .*

I'm as harried as a stump-tailed
cow durin' fly season.

Told You So

"You don't want to do any business with that Jake," Elmer told his friend Trace. "He's slicker than a leaky oil pan. Heck, he could steal the buttons off the long johns you're wearin' and sell 'em back to you as rare coins."

"Ain't that the gospel," said Elmer. "Why, just last week, I was over at Jake's place, spittin' nails and carryin' on. I hollered, 'Jake, you no-good snake in the grass, that mule you sold me is half-near blind!'

"And Jake says, 'I told you before you bought him, he was a fine mule, but didn't look good.'"

Bad Boss

He's been chased through the forest of mean and hit every tree trunk.

If you're warning your co-worker not to cross the boss, you might say . . .

He'll get mad enough to run a stray dog off a meat wagon.

Overworked

I'm so overworked, I'm busier than a funeral home fan in August.

When work is piling up, you might say . . .

I've got more tobacco than I can chew.

Cheapskate Boss

He's so tight that when he blinks,
his toes curl.

*If you're complaining that your
stingy boss won't give you a raise,
you might say . . .*

He's tighter than bark on a tree.

Doing Your Share

Them that don't pluck don't
get chicken.

*Referring to a co-worker who doesn't
pull his weight, you might say . . .*

They call him "Blister" 'cause he
don't show up 'til the work is done.

71

Forcing His Hand

Luke was having a hard time living up to his promise to his wife not to drink any more corn liquor.

One day as he was driving back from town, he stopped and picked up a hitchhiker who was fixing to visit his granny. No sooner did the young man get seated in the pickup than Luke pulled a gun on him and ordered him to get the jar of moonshine out of the glove compartment. "Take a big swig," Luke said, waving the gun.

The frightened hitchhiker took a gulp and darn near gagged to death.

But he was shocked even more after what happened next: Luke handed him the gun and said, "Now you take the gun and force me to take a drink."

Busy

I'm always so busy you'd
think I was twins.

*If you're going to have a busy day,
you might say . . .*

I got so much to do, I've got
to work early 'cause early
don't last long.

Bad Boss

He's meaner than a fryin' pan
full of rattlesnakes.

*If your boss keeps yelling at you,
you might think . . .*

If you keep whippin' the horse
back into the barn, he'll finally kick
you.

Hard Work

Grass don't grow on a busy street.

*If someone asks you the secret of your
success, you might say . . .*

Gardens ain't made by sittin'
in the shade.

Unfinished Work

You need to go back to the
chicken pen and start scratchin'.

*If your co-worker is stalling over
completing a task, you might say . . .*

Time to paint your butt white
and run with the antelope.

Overwhelmed

I feel like a short dog in tall grass.

*When a co-worker doubts that you can
get the job done, you might say . . .*

I ain't as good as I once was, but
I'm as good once as I ever was.

Good Worker

He can haul a sawed log
to hell and back.

*If you're describing a co-worker who
uses more brains than brawn,
you might say . . .*

A sharp ax is better than
big muscles.

Completing a Job

If you want the job done in time,
you better light a shuck.

*If you want to do a job in a perfunctory
fashion, you might say . . .*

We ain't got time to do it right,
so just hit it a lick and give it
a promise.

Busy

I'm busier than a set of jumper
cables at a family reunion.

*If you have too many things to deal with
at once at work, you might say . . .*

I'm weedin' a pretty wide row.

Big Shot

Otis staggered into the doctor's house and, pointing to his blood-soaked chest, said, "Hey, Doc, can you patch me up?"

"What happened to you?" Doc asked with alarm.

"My cousin Sully shot me."

"Why?"

"Well, me and the boys was havin' a good time drinkin', when Sully picked up his shotgun and said, 'Who wants to go huntin' with me?'"

"And then what happened?"

"I stood up and said, 'Sure, I'm game.'"

LOVE LEAVES YOU GRINNIN' LIKE A MULE EATIN' SAW BRIARS

(And Other Gospel Truths 'bout Love and Marriage)

Unusual Choice
for a Spouse

There's a lid to fit every skillet.

*If a friend married above his station,
you might say . . .*

He was raised on firebread and
soppin' gravy. She was raised
on ham and eggs.

Romance

- - - - - - - - - - - - - - - - - -

If women were flowers,
I'd pick you.

*If you're in a romantic mood,
you might tell your honey . . .*

That moon is pretty enough
to make a rabbit smooch a
hound dog.

Divorce

Looks like them two will end up
splittin' the blanket.

*If you're talking about the end of a
relationship, you might say . . .*

Breakin' up hits you up side
the head and leaves you down
in the mouth.

Compliment

Well, don't you look prettier
than a pat of butter meltin' on
a short stack.

*If your honey asks, "How do you like
my new perfume?" you might say . . .*

You stink pretty.

Warning to Husbands

Don't buy anythin' with
a handle on it, 'cause it can
only lead to work.

*Talking about husbands trying
to understand their wives,
you might say . . .*

Any man tryin' to figure out
a woman ends up as confused
as a cow in a parkin' lot.

Magic Doors

On their first visit to the big city, Dilbert, his wife, Deanna, and their son, Dewey, enter a huge department store for the first time. Dilbert and Dewey walk around in awe while Deanna goes off to shop for some unmentionables.

Dilbert and Dewey are wide-eyed by the wonders of the place, especially by two shiny, silver walls that move apart and then slide back together.

"Paw," Dewey asks, "what's that?"

Dilbert shakes his head. "I dunno, son. I ain't never seen anythin' like it."

While the two watch in amazement, an ugly, overweight woman waddles up to the moving walls and presses a button. The walls open and she steps into a small room. The walls close. Father and son watch the numbers above the walls light up: one, two, three, four. A few seconds later: three, two, one. Then the walls open up and out struts a stunning blonde so pretty that the sight knocks the clay right off of their boots.

Not taking his eyes off the beauty, Dilbert whispers to his son, "Dewey, go get your momma."

Marriage

Marriage is just like sittin'
in a bathtub. Once you get
used to it, it ain't so hot.

*If you're talking about the secret to a
happy marriage, you might say . . .*

Life is simpler when you plow
'round the stumps.

Hard-to-Please Woman

She's so persnickety, she wouldn't be happy in a diamond mine.

Speaking about a wife who's extremely fussy, you might say . . .

When she gets to heaven, she's gonna ask for better accommodations.

Lousy Husband

He's the kind of man who tells his wife, "I can't do all that work 'cause I got a bone in my leg."

Referring to a woman who married a loser, you might say . . .

She sure got the short end of the stick.

Living in Sin

Now, there's a couple that ate supper before they said grace.

If you admit that you had premarital sex, you might say . . .

We planted the corn before the fence was built.

It's All Relative

Tommy Lee and Katy Lynn had been married just long enough for the new to wear off, so now they were getting under each other's skin. One day while they were driving to see her parents, they were arguing in the car. As they drove past a barnyard full of pigs and jackasses, Tommy couldn't resist saying, "Relatives of yours?"

"Yep," says Katy Lynn, without skipping a beat. "My in-laws."

Love-Struck

I'm as happy as a goat in a briar patch.

If you're talking about how deeply in love you are, you might say . . .

I'm as happy as if I had good sense.

Disagreements

Arguin' with her is like a bug arguin' with a chicken.

If your spouse says something inflammatory during an argument, you might think . . .

That's puttin' the fat in the fire.

Compliment

You look prettier than a
store-bought doll.

*Referring to a beautiful woman,
you might say . . .*

She's prettier than a little red
wagon full of speckled pups.

Cursed

At the county fair, old man Homer slipped into the tent of the carnival fortune-teller and asked her, "Can you remove a curse I've been living with for the last forty years?"

The fortune-teller fingered the beads around her neck and studied Homer for a minute before answering, "Of course I can. But you have to tell me the exact words that were used to put the curse on you."

"That's not a problem," Homer declared. "I remember it like it was yesterday. The exact words were, 'I now pronounce you man and wife.'"

Two-Timer

He's as low as a snake in
a wagon track.

*If your friend is trying to cover up his
affair after being spotted with his
mistress, you might say . . .*

You can hide the fire, but what're
you gonna do with the smoke?

Beautiful Woman

I'd like to walk her to the
front row.

*If you're talking about a woman who
ages well, you might say . . .*

She's a spittin' image of herself.

Flirting

Flirtin' with a married woman
is as safe as if you were in
Abraham's back pocket and
him fixin' to sit down.

*Warning your married friend about
flirting, you might say . . .*

It's like tryin' to lick honey off a
blackberry vine — it looks temptin'
but you're just gonna get all cut up.

Choosing the Right Spouse

If you don't want blisters on your butt, ride a good saddle.

If you want to compliment a man on his choice for a wife, you might say . . .

You sure didn't pick up no crooked stick.

Chatterbox Wife

She'd talk the ears off a dead mule.

To a wife who can't stop talking, you might say . . .

You better stand up, 'cause you're talkin' the legs right off your chair.

Advice and Consent

Sally Ann had sweet eyes for Billy Bob, who didn't have a clue that she was smitten with him. The two were walking down a path from his house. He was loaded down with a washtub on his back, a live chicken under his arm, and a cane in his hand that he was using to lead a calf.

When they came to the woods, Sally Ann hesitated. She fluttered her baby blues and said coyly, "Billy Bob, I'm afraid to walk in there with you 'cause you just might try to steal a kiss."

He shook his head and said, "With all that I'm carryin', how could I possibly kiss you?"

"Well," Sally Ann replied, "you could stick that cane in the ground, tie the calf to it, and put the chicken under the washtub."

Husband
of Few Words

- - - - - - - - - - - - - - - - - -

He don't use his kindlin'
to start a fire.

*Referring to a husband who
acts cool because he hides his
emotions, you might say . . .*

There may be snow on the roof
but there's fire in the hearth.

Philanderer

Ask him no questions and he
won't tell you no lies.

*Referring to a friend who has fallen
for two women at the same time,
you might say . . .*

He's so confused, he don't know if
he's afoot or on horseback.

It Should Be
a Whopper

Junior climbed down from the sleeping loft and tiptoed into his parents' bedroom where his momma was reading one of those dime-store novels by candlelight.

"It's three in the mornin'," she said. "What in tarnation are you doin' in here?"

"I can't sleep, Momma. I was hopin' you could tell me a story."

She patted her bed and said, "Come and sit a spell with me, honey. When your darn-fool daddy comes home, he can tell us both one."

Loveless Marriage

She's as cold as a cast-iron toilet seat.

If you're not getting as much loving as you want, you might say . . .

I'm as frustrated as a rooster in an empty henhouse.

Smooth Talker

Women need to keep him
at a distance — like they do
skunks and bankers.

*If women are swooning over a
slick operator, you might tell them . . .*

You might think he's the
genuine article, but he ain't
got no guarantee.

Great Catch for a Husband

He's bigger than life and twice as handsome.

If you're talking about a man who dotes on his wife, you might say . . .

He carries her on a silk pillow.

Love-Struck

I'm as happy as a tick on a fat dog!

If you're acting goofy because you've fallen head over heels in love, you might say . . .

I'm so mixed up, I don't know daylight from dark.

Depraved Woman

She's so bad, she can make a preacher lay down his Bible.

If you're talking about a woman with loose morals, you might say . . .

They call her "Radio Station," 'cause any man can pick her up.

Morally Challenged Husband

He ain't fit to roll with the hogs.

*If you and your divorced friends are
trashing your ex-husbands,
you might say . . .*

Good men are as scarce as deviled
eggs after a church picnic.

Lousy Husband

He's as sorry as a two-dollar watch.

If you're talking about your bar-hopping husband, you might say . . .

Keepin' him home at night is as easy as puttin' socks on a rooster.

Posted

One day the wife passes on and they prepare the coffin and put her in it. The pallbearers start to take her to the church, but when they're going through the yard gate, they bump the coffin against a post and the old lady sits up, wide awake. They carry her back in the house and she lives for another ten years.

Finally, she passes on for sure. They get out the coffin, put her in it, and again the pallbearers start for the church. When they get near the gate, her husband cautions, "Now, boys, watch out for that post."

YOU'RE NOT WORTH THE SPIT IT'D TAKE TO CUSS YOU OUT

(And Other Digs and Cuts)

Dishonest

You lie so much, you have to hire someone to call in your dogs.

Gossiping

You ain't nothin' but a trash toter.

Ineffective

You're as useless as a milk bucket
under a bull.

Confused

You couldn't find your
own butt with two hands and a
search warrant.

A Bunch of Bull

An old farmer filed a lawsuit against the railroad, claiming that the two o'clock freight train that clickety-clacked through his field every day had likely turned his prize bull into burger meat. All the farmer wanted was to be paid the fair market value for his missing bull.

On the day of the trial, this young hotshot big-city lawyer for the railroad sweet-talked the farmer into settling out of court for half of what he was asking.

After the farmer signed the release and got his check, the lawyer just couldn't resist gloating and said, "I hate to tell you this, old man, but there was no way I could've won the case. The engineer was asleep and the fireman was in the caboose when you lost your bull. I didn't have a single witness to put on the stand. I was bluffing you."

The farmer nodded and said, "I hate to tell you this, young man, but there was no way I could've won the case. That dadgum bull came home this mornin'."

Ignorant

If you put your brain in a
matchbox, it would roll 'round like
a BB in a boxcar.

Dishonest

You're so crooked, you could
hide behind a corkscrew.

Vocally Challenged

You couldn't carry a tune
in a bucket.

Lying

Your tongue wags at both ends.

Arrogant

You're so stuck up, you'd
drown in a rainstorm.

Ignorant

If your brain was leather,
it wouldn't make a saddle for
a june bug.

Undependable

You're so worthless, the tide
wouldn't take you out.

Corrupt

You're so dishonest, you'd steal
the lard out of a biscuit.

Lazy

You wouldn't catch your breath
if it didn't come natural.

Morally Challenged

You're as crooked as a hound dog's
hind leg and twice as dirty.

Stupid

If dumb were dirt,
you'd be 'bout an acre.

Pessimistic

You're so negative,
you'd depress the devil.

Double Whammy

A Yankee comes down to visit his country folks, so naturally they drag him to church and introduce him to the preacher. After the service, the preacher stands at the door and shakes hands with the congregation.

"Well, Lord have mercy!" he declares upon seeing the visitor with two black eyes. "You didn't have those shiners when you came in. What happened to you?"

The Yankee winces and explains, "You remember the large lady that stood in front of me during the song service?"

The preacher nods.

"Well," says the Yankee, "I noticed her dress was wedged, so I reached over and pulled it out. That's when she clobbered me in the right eye."

The preacher shook his head in sympathy. "So what happened to your left eye?"

"She slugged me again."

"Why?"

"She was so angry at me for what I'd done, I tried to wedge her dress back in."

Intolerant

You're so narrow minded,
you can see through a keyhole
with both eyes.

Disorganized

You're so mixed up,
you couldn't organize a drinkin'
contest in a brewery.

Complaining

You're so ungrateful,
you'd gripe with a ham
under each arm.

Lazy

If you had a third hand,
you'd need another pocket
to put it in.

Scruffy

You look like the dog has been keepin' you hidden under the porch.

Corrupt

You're so crooked, no one can tell from your tracks whether you're comin' or goin'.

Deceitful

You're lyin' like a no-legged dog.

Inept

You're 'bout as handy as a
back pocket on a shirt.

Spineless

You're nothin' but an empty sack.

Fibbing

You're fuller than a tick that's
been suckin' on a dog all day.

Face to Face

Ella Mae isn't any bigger than a
cornstalk in June and has a face as
sweet as a moon pie. But, oh, Lordy,
what a mouth on that child.

She was down at the five-and-
dime, and all out of sorts because
her momma wouldn't buy her new
shoes. While her momma was trying
on a dress, Ella Mae sat on a bench
outside the dressing room and sulked
like a puppy whose bone was filched.

The pouty little girl began making
not-so-nice faces in the three-sided
mirror, when a refined woman
walked over to her and said, "You're
such a pretty little girl, you shouldn't

make those terrible faces. When I was your age I was told that if I made an ugly face, it would stay that way."

As quick as a whip, Ella Mae retorted, "Well, you can't say you weren't warned."

Ignorant

If you put your brain in a
hummingbird, it'd fly backward.

Lazy

You're too lazy to open an
umbrella when it rains.

Annoying

I wish you'd take a long walk
off a short pier.

If you bump into someone you don't like, you might say . . .

Anytime you happen to pass my house, I'd sure appreciate it.

♦ ♦ ♦

If someone is acting like a martyr, you might say . . .

Get down off that cross, 'cause someone else needs the wood.

♦ ♦ ♦

If you want to slam someone who judges others, you might say . . .

You need to clean up your own backyard before talkin' trash.

*If you want to threaten someone,
you might say . . .*

I'll knock a knot on your head
and dare it to rise.

♦ ♦ ♦

*If a salesman is giving you a line,
you might say . . .*

Our cow died last night,
so we don't need your bull.

♦ ♦ ♦

*If you're annoyed about receiving advice
from a hypocrite, you might say . . .*

I don't see no corn in your crib.

*If you're putting down someone
who's nothing but a big pretender,
you might say . . .*

You're all hat and no cattle.

♦ ♦ ♦

*To someone who takes way
too much time to complete a task,
you might say . . .*

You'd be the right feller to send for
the doctor if the devil was sick.

♦ ♦ ♦

*If you want to threaten someone,
you might say . . .*

I'll cut off your water and
take out the meter.

A Tight Situation

Between slopping the hogs, weeding
the beans, and chopping firewood,
Luanne had no reason to wear fancy
clothes. But every once in a while,
she liked to get gussied up for the
church socials and barn dances.

One day she came home with a
fancy store-bought dress and put it
on for her husband, Donny Joe, to
admire. Now, when she wasn't in
her dungarees, Luanne could show
off more curves than a mountain
creek. So, there in the bedroom, she
wriggled into her new dress and
asked Donny Joe, "What do you
think?"

"I'm a little confused," he said.

"How so, Donny Joe?"

He answered, "Are you outside tryin' to get in, or inside tryin' to get out?"

*To someone who is wild behind
the wheel, you might say . . .*

You're gonna cause a month's
worth of buryins.

♦ ♦ ♦

*To someone who acts arrogant
after inheriting a large sum of money,
you might say . . .*

The higher a monkey climbs,
the more he shows his butt.

♦ ♦ ♦

*If you're knocking someone
whose family has a history of lowlifes,
you might say . . .*

There're lots of nooses hangin'
in your family tree.

*If you're annoyed by someone
who likes the sound of his own voice,
you might say . . .*

You've got a ten-gallon mouth
and an elephant's ears.

♦ ♦ ♦

*If you want to threaten someone,
you might say . . .*

I'll cloud up and rain
all over you.

♦ ♦ ♦

*To a person who thinks he's a big shot,
you might say . . .*

I knew you when you weren't,
and you still ain't!

Flying in the Face
of the Law

A young country man named Jonas was driving his pickup, which was piled with manure, when he was pulled over by the sheriff.

"Boy, I'm writin' you a citation for carryin' too big of a load," said the sheriff.

As the lawman took out his pen, some of the flies accompanying the manure started to buzz him. He swatted and cussed at the flies.

"Them's circle flies," said Jonas. "We call 'em that 'cause back on the farm, they're always circlin' the horse's ass."

"Boy, are you calling me a horse's ass?" the sheriff growled.

"Oh, no, sir," said Jonas. "But you can't fool them flies."

HE'S AS SCARED AS A SINNER IN A CYCLONE

(And Other Look-Sees 'bout People)

Intelligent

She's as smart as a tree
full of owls.

Lazy

It's a sorry dog that won't wag
its own tail.

Spirited

She's livelier than a puppy
with two tails.

Exaggeration-Prone

He's full of more nuts and berries
than a fat bear.

Unintelligent

He won't hurt his back
totin' his brains.

Arrogant

They're so snooty that if they
get to heaven, they're gonna ask
to see the upstairs.

Strong

He's tougher than a
one-eared alley cat.

Pompous

That big mouth is all vine
and no taters.

Untrustworthy

You can shake his hand,
but count your fingers when
you're done.

Brilliant

If his brain were a rifle,
he'd shoot the stinger off a bee.

Stupid

His cheese slid off his cracker.

Holding On

The family threw a surprise birthday party for Grandma Clara—a real shindig with cake and ice cream and balloons. At the party, her grandson Jimmy asked her, "How old are you, Memaw?"

"Forty-nine and holdin'," Clara answered.

Jimmy thought a minute and said, "Memaw, how old would you be if you let go?"

Contrary

If you throwed her in the river,
she'd float upstream.

Dishonest

He'd steal anythin' that ain't
too hot or too heavy to carry.

Open-Minded

She don't wear no blinders.

Brainless

He doesn't have as much sense
as you could slap in a gnat's butt
with a butter paddle.

Egotisical

She thinks she's the only
huckleberry on the bush.

Anxious

He's as jumpy as a cockroach
in a fryin' pan.

Honorable

He plows straight and to the
end of the row.

Sluggish

He was born tired and raised lazy.

Snooty

She wouldn't make a vest out
of God's own overcoat.

Dependable

He's all wool and a yard wide.

Chatty

She gets tuckered out from
her own chin music.

Stingy

He's tighter than the skin
on a sausage.

148

Uppity

She's the honey, but the bees
don't know it.

Foul-Mouthed

His mouth ain't no prayer book.

Mmm, Mmm, Good

Church ladies from around the township held a luncheon at the restaurant where a group of wholesale liquor dealers were eating. At the end of the dealers' lunch, the men ordered a special dessert— watermelon soaked with brandy and rum.

To his horror, the restaurant owner discovered that there had been a mix-up, and the spiked melons had been served by mistake to the church ladies. "Did the women chew you out after they ate the wrong desserts?" he asked the head waiter.

"No, they didn't say a word," the waiter replied. "They was too busy throwin' the seeds from the melons in their purses."

Persistent

She'll stick to it 'til the last pea
is out of the pot.

Clueless

The engine is runnin' but ain't
nobody drivin'.

Honest

If he tells you that rooster
dips snuff, you can look under
its wing and find the can.

Egotistical

He thinks the sun comes up
just to hear him crow.

Elderly

He's two years older than dirt.

Selfish

She's so selfish, she wants the moon and the sun with two strands of barbed wire runnin' 'round 'em.

Unreliable

He sure ain't some boat you'd tie off to in a storm.

Small

She's littler than a bar of soap after a week's wash.

Vain

He breathes through his nose to keep from wearin' out his teeth.

Squandering

He's got a taste for champagne but a billfold for beer.

Gossiping

She has enough mouth for ten rows of teeth.

Confused

He don't know whether to scratch his watch or wind his butt.

Miserly

She's so stingy, she won't give you the time of day.

Drunk

He gets hisself so likkered up that he could throw himself on the ground and miss.

Overweight

She wears clothes so tight,
she looks like ten pounds
of potatoes in a five-pound sack.

Dull

He's about as sharp as
mashed potatoes.

Self-Centered

She wouldn't go to a funeral
unless she could be the corpse.

Unattractive

He's so ugly, his mama took him everywhere so she wouldn't have to kiss him good-bye.

Stupid

He couldn't pour rain out of a boot if the directions were written on the heel.

Stingy

He wouldn't pay a nickel to watch an ant pull a freight train.

Blind Faith

At church the other day, a good sister was swaying and dancing in the balcony, when she lost her balance and toppled clear over the railing. But, praise the Lord, her dress caught on the hanging light fixture, leaving her safely suspended but mighty exposed.

Thinking as quick as a rabbit in love, the preacher told the congregation, "The first man who looks at that fine Christian woman will be struck stone blind."

Sitting in the front pew, old Clyde covered half his face, looked up and told himself, "I reckon I can risk one eye."

Squandering

She can spend her paycheck
faster than a preacher can spot
a counterfeit nickel.

Clueless

Not only don't he know nothin',
he don't even suspect nothin'.

Stupid

He was behind the door when
they passed out the brains.

Honest

He's as straight as the
string on a kite.

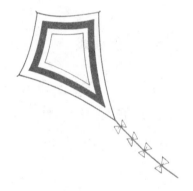

Dim-Witted

He's three pickles shy of a quart.

Unattractive

He's so ugly, his cooties
have to close their eyes.

Sad

She looks as happy as a
mule with a mouth full
of bumblebees.

Unintelligent

He's as dull as a
widow woman's ax.

Dinner to Die For

A married couple from up north decided to try a restaurant in a small Southern town and dined on fried chicken.

When they finished, the woman told the waitress, "That was simply delicious. Please, miss, would you tell us how you prepare your chickens?"

After a short pause, the waitress replied, "Well, ma'am, around here we don't do anything real special. We just tell 'em straight out: 'You're gonna die.'"

Egotistical

She thinks she's all that and
a bowl of grits.

Dense

He acts like he took the late train
and came in on the caboose.

Uptight

She's wound up tighter than
an eight-day clock.

Corrupt

He's as crooked as a
barrel full of snakes.

Unattractive

She ain't exactly ugly. She just
looks better from a distance.

Angry

He's as mad as a bear with
a sore butt.

Squandering

She spends money faster than
green grass goes through a goose.

Unwanted

He's as welcome as a skunk
at a church picnic.

Useless

He's as useful as a pogo stick
in quicksand.

A Doggone Shame

A traveling salesman drives up to a cabin in the woods and sees a barefoot child on the porch whittling a stick. A hound dog is laying in the yard.

"Hey, squirt, does your fleabag bite?" the salesman asks.

The boy replies, "Nope."

So the salesman steps out of his car. The hound runs over, snarling and growling, and bites him on his arms and legs. As the salesman is flailing around in the dust, he squeals to the boy, "I thought you said your dog doesn't bite!"

"It doesn't," said the boy. "But this here dog ain't mine."

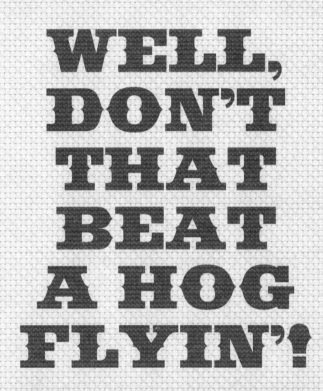

WELL, DON'T THAT BEAT A HOG FLYIN'!

(And Other Hoots and Hollers)

If you want to compliment a cook,
you might say . . .

Boy! That tasted like more!

♦ ♦ ♦

If someone asks about how sick you are,
you might say . . .

I'd have to get better just to die.

♦ ♦ ♦

If someone is trying to con you,
you might say . . .

Don't pee down my leg and tell
me it's rainin'.

*When someone is mad at you,
you might say . . .*

Who licked the red off your
candy?

♦ ♦ ♦

*If something seems pointless,
you might say . . .*

That juice ain't worth the
squeezin'!

♦ ♦ ♦

When it's time to eat, you might say . . .

Let's get greasy 'round the mouth.

♦ ♦ ♦

*If you receive some bad news,
you might say . . .*

Well, don't that just dill my pickle!

If someone is beating around the bush, you might say . . .

Hurry up and get to the tail of the dog.

♦ ♦ ♦

If someone tells you something that you totally agree with, you might say . . .

If that ain't the truth, then grits ain't groceries and eggs ain't poultry.

♦ ♦ ♦

If you're explaining something obvious for the third time, you might say . . .

You're still lookin' at me like a calf at a new gate.

I'll Drink to That

During a recent hot spell, Uncle Zeke collapses on the street in front of the general store. Several townsfolk rush over to see what they can do.

"Give the poor man a drink of whiskey," a little old lady says.

"Give him some air," says the mailman.

"Give the poor man a drink of whiskey," the elderly woman says again.

"Give him some water," says the schoolteacher.

While several other folks give suggestions, Uncle Zeke sits up and hollers, "Will y'all shut up and listen to the little ol' lady?"

*When asked if you're going to attend
a party, you might say . . .*

Yep, if the good Lord's willin' and
the creek don't rise.

♦ ♦ ♦

*If you're tired of repeating the same
thing, you might say . . .*

I don't chew my tobacco twice.

♦ ♦ ♦

*If you're in an argument with
someone who's starting to lose control,
you might say . . .*

Don't go off with your
pistol half-cocked.

When something is for certain,
you might say . . .

Is a frog's butt watertight?

◆ ◆ ◆

When asked how your day is going,
you might say . . .

As fine as snuff and not
half as dusty.

◆ ◆ ◆

To a person who makes a statement
that leaves you scratching your head,
you might say . . .

That makes as much sense as
a trapdoor in a canoe.

*If you're talking about a great meal
you just ate, you might say . . .*

That food was so good, it'd make
a body slap his grandma.

♦ ♦ ♦

*If you just hit your thumb with a
hammer, you might say . . .*

It'll feel better when it
quits hurtin'.

♦ ♦ ♦

*If someone isn't making much sense,
you might say . . .*

Man, your shirt is missin'
a few buttons.

*If someone came up with a bad idea,
you might say . . .*

That notion will go over like a
frog in the punch bowl.

◆ ◆ ◆

*If you're at a function that has left
you bored, you might say . . .*

I've had fun before, and this
ain't it!

◆ ◆ ◆

*If you skipped breakfast and lunch,
you might say . . .*

I'm so hungry, my belly's gonna
sue my teeth for nonsupport.

If you're looking for answers in all the wrong places, you might say . . .

I might as well be fishin'
in the clouds.

♦ ♦ ♦

*If you don't have an opinion
while listening to a debate between
other friends, you might say . . .*

I ain't got no dog in this race.

♦ ♦ ♦

*If you come up with a great idea,
you might say . . .*

It's horse high, bull strong, pig
tight, and gooseproof.

*If you want to compliment the cook,
you might say . . .*

Supper was so good, it makes me
want to swallow my tongue so I
can eat my taste buds.

◆ ◆ ◆

*If you have some gossip you want
to dish out, you might say . . .*

I'm not one to go 'round spreadin'
rumors, so you better listen close
the first time.

◆ ◆ ◆

*If you're in agreement with someone,
you might say . . .*

We're both sittin' in amen corner.

In No Hurry

The preacher man meets Moody on the path toward the church, and after exchanging small talk, says, "Do you want to go to heaven?"

Moody's eyes get big and he shakes his head. "No, preacher."

The preacher man is confounded and asks again, "Are you sure you don't want to go to heaven when you die?"

Moody nods this time and says, "Oh, sure, preacher—when I die. I thought you was gettin' a party to go now."

If someone is chewing you out,
you might say . . .

Oh, don't get your tail up and
stinger out!

◆ ◆ ◆

If a friend boasts about completing
a task that most anyone could do,
you might say . . .

It's easy gettin' off a buckin' mule.

◆ ◆ ◆

If your friend tells you that he's being
audited by the IRS, you might say . . .

That'll put a quiver in your liver.

When someone gets to the heart of the matter, you might say . . .

You done chewed the bark
off the tree.

♦ ♦ ♦

If you find yourself with a serious problem, you might say . . .

Now, ain't this a fine howdy-do.

♦ ♦ ♦

If you don't care one way or the other, you might say . . .

I don't have no knives
to sharpen.

In answer to something that's obvious,
you might say . . .

Does a cat have climbin' gear?

♦ ♦ ♦

To someone who is being evasive,
you might say . . .

You're beatin' the devil
'round the stump.

♦ ♦ ♦

If you promise to do something,
but want to leave some wiggle room,
you might say . . .

I'll do it, if nothin' breaks
or comes untwisted.

*If you're amazed by some
unexpected event, you might say...*

Next thing you know, the hoot
owls will be flirtin' with the
chickens.

♦ ♦ ♦

If you're sick, you might say...

I was better, but I got over it.

♦ ♦ ♦

If you missed lunch, you might say...

I'm so hungry, I could eat the
south end of a northbound mule.

♦ ♦ ♦

*If you are absolutely certain,
you might say...*

As sure as rats run the rafters.

The Right Number

After a few years of home schooling, Johnny shows up for the first time for class at a public school. The teacher explains to him that he can't go to the washroom unless he raises two fingers.

The boy looks puzzled and asks, "Uh, ma'am, how's that gonna stop it?"

If you're ordering someone out of your house, you might say . . .

Don't let the door hit you where the Lord split you.

♦ ♦ ♦

If you want to encourage people to say what they really think, you might say . . .

There's more room out than there is in.

♦ ♦ ♦

If your favorite team won big, you might say . . .

They sure cleaned them boys' plows.

If you hear a bad idea,
you might say . . .

That makes as much sense as
tryin' to sling a hammock
'tween two cornstalks.

♦ ♦ ♦

When the family sits down to
a big feast, you might say . . .

Ya'll be careful now,
or you're gonna fleshen up.

♦ ♦ ♦

If someone is speaking with great
passion, you might say . . .

Tell the truth and shame the devil!

Location, Location, Location

The traveling salesman stepped off the train and frowned when he learned that the town was a far piece down the road. "Why in the name of Moses did they put the depot so far from town?" he asked Clinton, one of the locals.

"Well, stranger," said Clinton, "it's probably 'cause they wanted it as close to the tracks as possible."

*If a friend is setting unrealistic goals,
you might say . . .*

You're hangin' your basket higher
than you can reach.

♦ ♦ ♦

*If someone is beating around the bush,
you might say . . .*

You're takin' the long way
'round the barn.

♦ ♦ ♦

*If a friend is planning to do something
dumb and dangerous, you might say . . .*

You might as well pick your teeth
with a rattlesnake.

*To emphatically agree with
someone's opinion, you might say . . .*

If that ain't a fact,
God's a possum.

◆ ◆ ◆

*If a friend made a big mistake like
breaking up or quitting a job,
you might say . . .*

You sure dropped your candy.

◆ ◆ ◆

*To a big gossip hound,
you might say . . .*

Keep my name out of your mouth.

When you hear some disturbing news, you might say . . .

Well, that sure jars my preserves!

♦ ♦ ♦

If you're referring to the time you got the last word in an argument, you might say . . .

I sure preached his funeral.

♦ ♦ ♦

If you've overeaten, you might say . . .

I've had more than a plenty.

*If you think someone has the
wrong facts, you might say . . .*

You're sniffin' in the wrong hole.

♦ ♦ ♦

*To someone who has reached the
wrong conclusion, you might say . . .*

You're drivin' your chickens to
the wrong market.

♦ ♦ ♦

*If you're leaving it up to your spouse
to pick a movie, you might say . . .*

Your druthers is my druthers.

If you really don't feel like going out with friends, you might say . . .

I can't dance and it's too wet to plow.

♦ ♦ ♦

If you want to compliment someone's cooking, you might say . . .

This is gooder 'n grits!

♦ ♦ ♦

If you need someone to repeat what he just said, you might say . . .

Can you lick that calf again?

Snake's Alive!

Ol' Bud was catching bass at his favorite fishing hole when he spotted a water moccasin with a frog in its mouth. Bud knew big bass like frogs, so he decided to steal it from the snake.

He sneaked up behind the reptile and grabbed it around the head. Then he pried open the snake's mouth, yanked out the frog, and dropped it in his bait can.

Afraid that the water moccasin would bite him if he let it go, Ol' Bud reached into the back pocket of his bib overalls, pulled out a pint of moonshine, and poured a good amount into the snake's mouth. The water moccasin's eyeballs rolled back and its body went limp. So Bud tossed the snake into the water and went back to fishing.

A few minutes later, Bud felt something rubbing against his bare toe. He looked down and couldn't believe what he was seeing. There was that water moccasin again, only this time it had two frogs in his mouth!

*If you hear something that leaves
you exasperated, you might say . . .*

Well, don't that put pepper
in my gumbo!

♦ ♦ ♦

*If you're getting needled because you're
losing at a game, you might say . . .*

Church ain't over 'til the choir
stops singin'.

♦ ♦ ♦

*If it's time to end the party,
you might say . . .*

Time to pee on the fire and
call in the dogs.

Ham-Handed

Fannie goes to see the governor and pleads, "Can you get my husband out of the penitentiary?"

"What's he in for?" the governor asks.

"Stealin' a ham."

"That doesn't sound so bad. Is he a good man?"

"Not really," Fannie admits. "He's a lazy worker and he's mean to me and the kids."

"Then why in blazes do you want a man like that out of prison?"

"'Cause we're out of ham."

If you're surprised by what you've just heard, you might say . . .

Well, pick my peas!

Or

Well, tie me to an anthill
and fill my ears with jam!

Or

Well, tie me to a pig and
roll me in the mud!

Or

Well, don't that cock your pistol!

Or

Well, don't that knock your hat
in the creek!

Or

Well, slap my head and
call me stupid!

Or

Well, don't that put the tassel
on my cap!

Or

Well, butter my butt and
call me a biscuit!

SPARKIN' AN' SPOONIN'

(Notions 'bout Datin')

Fun

*If you're telling someone about
the great evening you had
with your date at the dance,
you might say . . .*

We had ourselves a hog-killin' time.

Anticipation

*To someone wondering how an upcoming
date will turn out, you might say . . .*

You can never tell which way the
pickle's gonna squirt.

Charisma

Speaking about a guy who swept a girl off her feet with a romantic gesture, you might say . . .

He sure bowled that maiden over.

Anxiety

If you're going out on a highly anticipated date for the first time, you might say . . .

I'm as nervous as a mama cow with a bucktoothed calf.

Competition

*In advising a really nice guy
who's wondering if he should compete
against a stud athlete
for the attentions of a gal,
you might say . . .*

If you can't sing, dance.

Hearsay

*If you're hearing wild rumors
about a girl you want to date,
you might say . . .*

Them's the kinda things a fella
likes to find out for himself.

Some Surprise

A country boy walks up to the perfume counter at Woolworth's and tells the clerk he'd like a bottle of perfume for his girlfriend's birthday.

The clerk smiles and says, "You're gonna surprise her, huh?"

"Yep," he answers. "She's expectin' a diamond ring."

Knowledge

*To a girl who's agreed to go out with
a fellow she knows nothing about,
you might say . . .*

Never test the depth of the water
with both feet.

Rejection

*To someone who turned down a date
with a good-looking nice guy,
you might say . . .*

The piece of pie you pass up is
the piece you'll never get.

Yearning

*If you have a strong desire or
longing to ask out a certain girl,
you might say . . .*

I've got a hankerin' to call on her.

Risk

*To a friend who's planning to date
a woman known as a man-killer,
you might say . . .*

Careful is the naked man climbin'
a barbwire fence.

Antique Appraisal

Two young country girls meet for coffee one Saturday morning. "How was your blind date?" Raylene asks Betty Jo.

"Awful!" Betty Jo answers. "He showed up in a 1956 Ford pickup."

"The truck is a classic. What's so bad about that?"

Betty Jo sighs and explains, "He's the original owner."

Enchantment

To the person you've fallen for after a couple of dates, you might say . . .

Are your legs tired, 'cause you've been runnin' through my dreams.

Scoundrel

In advising a gal who's wondering if she should go out with a fellow who has a reputation as a cad, you might say . . .

It don't take no genius to spot a goat in a flock of sheep.

Spendthrift

Warning a friend who tries to impress his woman by showering her with jewelry, you might say . . .

Broke is what happens when you let your yearnin's get ahead of your earnin's.

Age

To those wondering why a gal would be dating someone much older than her, you might say . . .

The old pipe gives the sweetest smoke.

The Perfect Companion

At the church social, a young woman tells her friend about her idea of the perfect mate: "The fellow I marry must be a shinin' light. He must be musical, tell jokes, sing, and stay home at night."

Overhearing the conversation, the old church lady pipes up, "Sugar, if that's all you want, get a TV."

Uncertainty

*In advising a friend who is concerned
that he's falling for a girl and isn't sure
what to do about it, you might say . . .*

Ride the horse in the direction
it's goin'.

Perseverance

*To a woman who's losing faith that she
will ever fall for the right man,
you might say . . .*

You have to kiss a lot of toads
before you find your prince.

Character

When describing a date with
a genuine, polite, trustworthy guy,
you might say . . .

He's a true copper-bottomed
gentleman.

Suspicion

As a warning to a fellow whose
girlfriend works with his good-looking,
womanizing brother, you might say . . .

You can't trust your dog to watch
your food.

Since You Asked . . .

After a minor tiff, Joe Don tells his girlfriend Priscilla, "I don't know how God could have made you so stupid yet so beautiful."

"I'd be tickled to explain," says Priscilla. "God made me beautiful so you would be attracted to me. God made me stupid so I would be attracted to you."

Fatal Attraction

Laura Beth and Dicky Ray went on a blind date that was a disaster from the start. No chemistry, no compatibility, no meaningful conversation. Earlier, Laura Beth had secretly arranged to have a friend call her at the diner so she would have an excuse to leave if something like this happened.

To her relief, the friend phoned the eatery and Laura Beth took the call. When she returned to the table, she dabbed her eyes and told Dicky Ray, "I have some bad news. My grandfather just died."

"Thank heavens," Dicky Ray replied. "If yours hadn't, mine would have had to."

Jeopardy

- - - - - - - - - - - - - - - - - -

*Advising someone who is
planning on dating a person known
to create havoc with the heart,
you might say . . .*

You can't keep trouble from
comin', but you don't have to
give it a chair to sit on.

Cruising

- - - - - - - - - - - - - - - - - -

*If you and your buddies are
looking for girls to go out with,
you might say . . .*

Let's go sparrow catchin'.

Impression

In describing a fellow who's going all out to make a big hit with a young woman, you might say . . .

He's tryin' to make a mash
on that girl.

Delusion

To a gal who's deceiving herself into thinking that she'll be asked out by a guy who everyone knows is in love with someone else, you might say . . .

You're flyin' away with the fairies.

Rejection

*To a guy who has been
turned down time and again
for a date with a certain girl,
you might say . . .*

You're barkin' at a knot.

Uncertainty

*If you're talking to a gal who's
not so sure about her feelings
for her once-hot boyfriend,
you might say . . .*

You didn't fall in love; you just
tripped over it.

Late Night

After waiting at the restaurant for more than an hour and a half for her date, Mary Sue figured she had been stood up. She went home, slipped into her pajamas and slippers, fixed a bowl of popcorn, and began watching a rerun of *Hee Haw*.

No sooner had she plopped down in front of the TV when her doorbell rang. There stood her date, Elmer. He took one look at her and gasped, "Gosh and tarnation! I'm two hours late . . . and you still ain't ready?"

Gaffe

*To a friend who realized she
had accidentally made dates with
two guys for the same night,
you might say . . .*

You're in one all-fired bad box.

Rendezvous

*Speaking about being asked on
a date by the most eligible bachelor
in town, you might say . . .*

I'm steppin' out with the biggest
toad in the pond.

Bad Judgment

About a gal who constantly goes out with the wrong guys, you might say . . .

She don't make mistakes.
She just dates 'em.

Personality

In describing the allure of a recent date, you might say . . .

She could charm the dew right off the honeysuckle.

Attraction

Talking about a fellow you're smitten with, you might say . . .

Every time I'm with him,
I get more butterflies than a
field full of petunias.

Frustration

*If you've dated lots of women
without finding the right one,
you might say . . .*

I sowed wild oats and reaped
prunes and bran.

Appearance

*Advising a gal who's concerned
that the nice guy she's dating isn't very
handsome, you might say . . .*

A good horse is never
a bad color.

Brashness

*To a fellow who always comes on much
too strong to the women he meets, you
might say . . .*

A lasso ain't no datin' tool.

Free Spirit

- -

*Talking about the madcap girl
you're dating who follows the beat of a
different drummer, you might say . . .*

Oh, lordy, is she a caution!

Prudence

- -

*Warning a friend who's infatuated with
someone with a questionable reputation,
you might say . . .*

If you've fallen in love at first sight,
you better look twice.

Attraction

In seeing a sexy woman flirt with your buddy, you might say . . .

She's battin' her eyes at you like a toad in a hailstorm.

Good Guy

If you're talking about the nice guy you dated last night, you might say . . .

There are few weevils in his cotton.

Honest-to-Goodness Real Country Songs

She Feels Like a
New Man Tonight

The Last Word in Lonesome
Is "Me"

How Can You Believe Me When
I Say I Love You, When You
Know
I've Been a Liar All My Life?

All the Guys Who Turn Me On
Turn Me Down

How Come Your Dog Don't Bite
Nobody But Me?

High Cost of Low Living

Run for the Roundhouse, Nellie
(He Can't Corner You There)

If You Don't Believe I Love You
(Ask My Wife)

♥ ♥ ♥

She's Looking Better Every Beer

♥ ♥ ♥

My Shoes Keep Walking
Back to You

♥ ♥ ♥

If My Nose Was Running Money,
Honey (I'd Blow It All on You)

♥ ♥ ♥

I'll Dance at Your Wedding
(If You'll Marry Me)

Sex

*Advising a fellow who views
his dates as sex objects,
you might say . . .*

All that comes from a cow
ain't just milk.

Cause and Effect

*If your friend complains that
every guy she goes out with is a loser,
you might say . . .*

When you plant taters,
you get taters.

Improbability

Talking about an uncouth, unemployed fellow who plans to ask the town beauty out on a date, you might say . . .

He has no more chance than a grasshopper in a chicken house.

Slut

In describing a woman with a bad reputation, you might say . . .

Men pass her around like a mess of corn bread.

Womanizer

If you're warning your friend against going out with a slick, smooth-talking Lothario, you might say . . .

The devil can quote scripture
for his own ends.

Appearance

*To those who wonder why
a good-looking guy is dating
a plain-looking gal,
you might say . . .*

The eyes ain't responsible
for what the heart sees.

Excuse

*If your date stood you up and
then came up with a cockamamie reason
why he couldn't call you ahead of time,
you might say . . .*

Your excuse is as weak as
day-old dishwater.

Misfortune

*Talking about a fellow who keeps
striking out in the dating game,
you might say . . .*

He's gettin' nothin' but warm beer
and cold kisses.

Good Date

- - - - - - - - - - - - - - - - - - -

*In describing how much you enjoyed
a date that went better than expected,
you might say . . .*

It was too fine for nice,
but it was great for good.

Immaturity

- - - - - - - - - - - - - - - - - - -

*If you're talking about the
twenty-something you're dating
who still acts like a teenager,
you might say . . .*

He's between hay and grass.

Attentiveness

To those who wonder why an average-looking guy gets dates with the most sought-after girls, you might say . . .

The fragrance always stays on the hand that gives the rose.

Attraction

Of a man who is smitten by a certain woman, you might say . . .

He's taken a shine to her.

Closeness

Talking about a couple who are always together, you might say . . .

Them two are as thick as hair
on a dog's back.

Gentility

*In describing how classy your
date was, you might say . . .*

He was a gentleman of the
first water.

Solicitude

In complaining about a gal who is incredibly nice to the point of excess, you might say . . .

She's so sweet she's givin' me a toothache.

Appeal

To a guy you really like but are playing coy with, you might say . . .

If you rope me, you can have me.

Allure

In describing a woman who is doing all she can to win the affections of a certain man, you might say . . .

She's set her cap for him.

Enchantment

Talking about someone who's fallen fast and hard after a few dates, you might say . . .

It's plain as the tail on a rattler that she's sweet on him.

PITCHIN' WOO

(Say-Sos 'bout Courtin')

Infatuation

*If you're falling in love with
your sweetie pie, you might say . . .*

I'm soft down on you.

Happiness

*If you're head-over-heels in love,
you might say . . .*

If I were any peachier,
I'd be a cobbler.

Fear

*To a friend who's too afraid to
tell his sweetheart that he's in love
with her, you might say . . .*

You ain't got a hair on your butt
if you don't tell her.

Poetry

*To a friend who wants to recite
his gal a love poem that he wrote,
you might say . . .*

It's like a haircut — good,
and you feel like a million bucks;
bad, and you hide your head
under your hat.

Enchantment

*About a couple who are madly
in love, you might say . . .*

Their hearts are a-poppin' like
the flowers in May.

Coziness

*If you're snuggled in the arms
of your sweetheart,
you might say . . .*

I'm as comfy as an egg under a
hen sittin' in a wool basket.

My, How Times Change

Newlywed Betty Lou was sitting in the chair at the beauty parlor having her hair done and chattering happily about her new hubby. "He's everything I could hope for," she gushed. Then she rattled off a mess of good traits.

Violet, the beautician, who was on her third stormy marriage, cleared her throat and said, "Funny thing about new husbands. The same qualities that attracted you to him in the first place are usually the very ones you can't stand a year later."

Appearance

To people wondering how a beauty queen could fall in love with a less than handsome man, you might say . . .

Love is a great beautifier.

Absence

If you're apart from your honey for an extended period, you might say . . .

Life without you is like a rosebush without flowers.

Goofiness

If you're talking about a gal who's acting silly because she's smitten, you might say . . .

Ain't no cure for a girl in love.

Closeness

Talking about a lovey-dovey twosome who snuggle everywhere they go, you might say . . .

Now there goes a couple that's hip to haunch and cheek to jowl.

Long-Term Effect

Dixie woke up during the night to find her husband, Luke, wasn't in bed. She put on her robe, went downstairs, and found him sitting at the kitchen table with a double shot of moonshine in front of him. He was staring at the wall, wiping a tear from his eye.

"Why are you down here at this time of night, Luke?" she asked. "What's the matter?"

"Do you recollect twenty years ago when you were only sixteen and I was courtin' you?" he asked.

"Sure I do," she replied.

"And do you recollect that night your father caught us in the back of my pickup doin' the bump and grind?"

"Of course."

"Then you recollect him shovin' his shotgun in my face and yellin', 'Either you marry my daughter or spend the next twenty years in jail'?"

Dixie nodded.

Luke wiped another tear from his cheek and whined, "I would have been released today."

Fear

*To a guy who's afraid to tell his
girlfriend how much he loves her,
you might say . . .*

You ain't never gonna break
a horse if you stay sittin'
on the fence.

Love

*If you want to tell your
sweetie pie how much you're
in love, you might say . . .*

I love you more than a cat
loves the cream jar.

Sure as corn bread goes
with greens, you're the answer
to my dreams.

You make me happier than
a pig in slop.

Sure as shootin', sure as hell,
you're the flowers in my dell.

♥ ♥ ♥

A hundred wagons can't haul
all the love I have for you.

♥ ♥ ♥

You make me happier
than a gopher in soft dirt.

♥ ♥ ♥

Sure as vines wind 'round
the stump, you're my darlin'
sugar lump.

♥ ♥ ♥

Baby doll, I wouldn't trade you
for a fatted cow.

If I could reach the stars
I'd pull one down for you.

Sure as rain clouds come in June,
you're the heavens, stars,
and moon.

I made a wish and you came true.

In your arms is my favorite
place to be.

Sure as creeks go 'round the bend,
my love for you knows no end.

Earth ain't so bad 'cause
I'm in heaven with you.

You're it as far as I can see.

♥ ♥ ♥

You're the onliest person
who holds the key that can
open my heart.

Sure as lightnin' goes with thunder,
without you I'd go asunder.

If I had a single flower for every
time I think about you, I'd get
lost in my garden.

You're the butter on my biscuit.

Sure as God made all this land,
you hold my heart in your hand.

Lovin' you is like drinkin'
hot cider—it makes me feel
warm all over.

Loveliness

*If you want to tell your
sugarplum how fetching she is,
you might say . . .*

You're prettier than a
blue-ribbon lamb on fair day.

You're as pretty as a spotted horse
in a pasture full of daisies.

Sure as taters grow in dirt,
you look sexy in my shirt.

If I had a nickel for every time
I saw a gal as pretty as you,
I'd have a nickel.

You're as lovely as crimson
and clover.

You're sweeter than mama's tea.

♥ ♥ ♥

You're cuter than a babe
in a blanket.

♥ ♥ ♥

Sure as flowers bloom in spring,
you are such a pretty thing.

♥ ♥ ♥

You're cuter than a heifer calf
in a pansy patch.

Hell on Earth

Late one night, Ruth Ann came home from a date with her boyfriend. Her crestfallen face was streaked with tears.

"You look as gloomy as a treed coon," said her mama. "What's wrong, darlin'?"

"Billy-Ray proposed to me tonight," Ruth Ann replied.

"Well, hush my mouth!" her mama shouted with joy. "Ain't that the bee's knees! So why the long wet face?"

"He don't believe there's a hell."

"Marry him anyway," advised her mama. "Between the two of us, we'll show him just how wrong he is."

Proposal

If you're hinting at marriage,
you might say . . .

We might could rest our heads
every night on the same pillow.

Won't you ride with me down
Honeymoon Lane?

I'm a-yearnin' to add a branch
to your family tree.

You're the gal I want to
row down the river with.

Let's lock our hearts together
and throw away the key.

GETTIN' HITCHED

(Musin's 'bout Weddin's)

Happy Groom

In describing the happy groom,
you might say . . .

He was grinnin' like a
skunk eatin' cabbage.

Food for Thought

A traveling dietician stops in an Appalachian hollow to discuss with the local hill people the importance of good nutrition. "Most of you here have eaten entirely too many fried foods high in fat and empty calories," she informs them. "Can anyone tell me the most dangerous food of all?"

Cletus raises his hand and answers, "Weddin' cake."

Happy Daze

At the rehearsal dinner, the groom-to-be's Uncle Bill walks up to him and says, "Congratulations, boy. You'll look back on this day and remember it as the happiest day of your life."

"But, Uncle Bill, I ain't gettin' hitched 'til tomorrow," his nephew says.

Replies Uncle Bill, "I know, boy, I know."

Cold Feet

To a friend who's getting cold feet an hour before the wedding, you might say . . .

When you're on a horse gallopin' off a cliff, it's too late to shout "Whoa!"

Sweet Ceremony

If you believe the old wives' tale that an exceptionally sweet wedding ceremony leads to an exceptionally sweet marriage, you might say . . .

A fine beginnin' makes a dandy endin'.

Reception Blessing

At the church hall supper after the wedding, you might say . . .

Bless the bride, bless the bowl, bless the biscuits, give 'em soul.

Questionable Choice

About a woman who married a man most people didn't approve of, you might say . . .

That butterfly flew 'round all the pretty flowers and landed on a cow pie.

Cold Feet

*To a friend who's getting cold feet
the night before the wedding,
you might say . . .*

Courage is bein' scared to death
and saddlin' up anyway.

Good Fortune

*Talking about the working class groom
who just married into a wealthy family,
you might say . . .*

He's got it made in the shade,
if the tree don't fall.

Love for Sale

During the wedding rehearsal, Bevis the groom approached the preacher with an unusual offer: "I'll give you one hundred bucks if you'll change the weddin' vows."

"What do you want me to do?" the preacher asked.

"When you get to the part where I'm supposed to promise to love, honor, obey, and be faithful to her forever, just leave that part out."

The preacher took the bribe.

The next day at the ceremony, it came time for the groom's vows. The preacher looked Bevis in the eye and said, "Will you promise to prostrate yourself before her, obey her every command and wish, serve her breakfast in bed every morning, and swear eternally before God and your lovely wife that you will not even look at another woman for as long as you both shall live?"

Stunned speechless, Bevis gulped and looked around. All eyes were on him. Feeling totally betrayed and too afraid to bolt from the altar, he squeaked out, "I will."

When the ceremony was over, the groom, whose shock had turned to anger, pulled the preacher aside and, through clenched teeth, hissed, "I thought we had a deal."

"We did," admitted the preacher. Returning the $100 that Bevis had given him the day before, the preacher whispered, "But the bride made me a better offer."

Sweet Ceremony

*In describing what a loving
and emotional wedding it was,
you might say . . .*

It'd bring a tear to a glass eye.

Cold Feet

*To a friend who's worried about
going through with the wedding,
you might say . . .*

A faint heart never filled a flush.

Beautiful Bride

About a beautiful bride,
you might say . . .

Grace was in her steps,
heaven in her eyes.

Happy Groom

If you're a happy groom,
you might say . . .

I'm plumb tickled to death to be
walkin' down the aisle of love.

Amazing Ceremony

*If you're enjoying the best
wedding you've ever attended,
you might say . . .*

I've been to three county fairs and
a hog butcherin' but I ain't never
seen nothin' like this before.

Happy Newlywed

*As you happily walk together out
of the church on your wedding day,
you might say . . .*

I've got the world by the tail
with a downhill pull.

Wedding Sympathy

*When seeing the groom walk
into the church, you might say . . .*

Well, that's the last real decision
he'll ever make.

Like Father, Like Son-in-Law

At the wedding, Jenny couldn't help but notice that her friend Rita, the mother of the bride, was sobbing throughout the entire ceremony.

Later as the reception was winding down and the newlyweds had left, Jenny went over to comfort Rita, whose cheeks were still wet from tears. Jenny told her, "You're not losin' a daughter, you're gainin' a son.

I had a chat with the groom and he reminds me so much of your husband. You know what they say: Girls tend to marry men who are like their fathers."

"I know," wailed Rita. "That's why I'm cryin'."

Old Wives' Tales

Vows sweetly spoken won't
ever be broken.

A lovely day, a lovely bride.

A weepin' bride will be a
laughin' wife.

A laughin' bride will be a
weepin' wife.

Marry in May, rue the day.

Marry in white,
always be right.

Marry in blue,
always be true.

Marry in brown,
live in town.

Marry in black,
don't look back.

Marry in green,
never be seen.

Marry in red,
wish you were dead.

WEARIN' THE YOKE

(Hoots an' Hollers 'bout Marriage)

Different Woman

*To a friend who complains that his wife
isn't the same person he had married,
you might say . . .*

Trouble with a milk cow is
she won't stay milked.

Big Trouble

*In advising your buddy who's about
to be in big trouble with his wife because
he was out late drinking with you,
you might say . . .*

When it's your butt that's about to
go for a ride, try havin' more
common sense than pride.

Fair Trade

Old Man Grady was dying, so his family stood around his deathbed and tried to comfort the farmer in his final hours. In a weary voice, he whispered to his wife, Darlene, "After I've left for the hereafter, I want you to marry Wade, the farmer over in the next county."

"No, I can't marry anyone after you," she protested.

"Dadgummit, woman, I insist!" he wheezed.

Perplexed, Darlene asked, "But why?"

With his final breath, Grady replied, "He cheated me in a horse trade."

Body of Evidence

Darryl's wife, Jo-Dee, was the jealous type. When he came home after a night of drinking with the boys, she carefully examined his jacket, looking for strands of a woman's hair. When she couldn't find any, she pitched a hissy fit anyway: "So now you're cheatin' on me with a bald-headed woman!"

The next night, Darryl went out again. When he returned, Jo-Dee sniffed him from head to toe, but she couldn't find any trace of perfume on him. Nevertheless, Jo-Dee had another conniption: "She's not only bald-headed, but she's too cheap to buy perfume!"

Solid Marriage

If you're describing an enviable relationship, you might say . . .

Their marriage is as strong
as a pine knot.

Bad Moment

*To a friend in a solid,
loving marriage who confided
that he and his wife had a spat,
you might say . . .*

Well, every day ain't Sunday.

Happy Home

*A sign over the door of a
happy home might say . . .*

Forever thine, forever mine,
forever ours.

Milquetoast Hubby

*Talking about a husband who
doesn't stand up to his harping wife,
you might say . . .*

Woe to the house where the hen
crows and the rooster keeps still.

Misplaced Interest

*To a married friend who spends way
too much time on his hobby,
you might say . . .*

Never give your horse more
attention than your wife, unless
you like sleepin' in the barn.

Intimate Bond

*In describing a marriage where the
couple is secure in their relationship,
you might say . . .*

Their bond is as comfy as a garden
hammock in the summer shade.

Roaming Husband

*If you're offering advice to a
friend whose husband is always seen
carousing without her,
you might say . . .*

A loose horse is always lookin'
for new pastures.

Tumultuous Twosome

*In talking about a passionate
couple that acts madly in love one
moment and shouts madly in
anger the next, you might say . . .*

Their marriage might have been
made in heaven, but so are thunder
and lightnin'.

Good Fortune

*When explaining how you've remained
married for so long,
you might say . . .*

We've stayed hitched all these
years by guess and by God.

Control Issues

*Advising a friend whose
husband makes all the decisions,
you might say . . .*

Just 'cause you're followin'
a well-marked trail don't mean
that whoever made it knows
where he's goin'.

Side Effects

Conway had been slipping in and out of a coma for several months, yet his devoted wife, Scarlett, stayed by his bedside every single day.

When he finally regained consciousness, he motioned for her to sit on his bed. As he held her hand, Conway said, "You've been with me through all the bad times. When I fell off the barn roof and broke my leg, you were there. When the tractor ran over me, you were there. When the farm failed, you were there. When we lost the house, you were there. Now my health is failin', yet you're still by my side."

Scarlett was leaning in to give him a kiss when he added, "I'm beginnin' to think you're bad luck!"

Gloomy Twosome

*In describing an unhappy couple,
you might say . . .*

That marriage is all
beer and skittles.

Anger Management

*In revealing one of the secrets
to a successful marriage,
you might say . . .*

Don't let the moon see your wrath.

Tough Decision

Advising a stay-at-home mom who is wondering whether to leave her husband, you might say . . .

Never take to sawin' on the branch that's supportin' you, unless you're bein' hung from it.

Rough Patches

As a reminder that every marriage has its bad moments, you might say . . .

There never is a lane so long that it don't have some hills and curves.

What's Not
to Like?

While Caleb and Dolly are weeding the garden, they get into a little cuss fight.

"You hate my mama; just admit it," Dolly snaps. "You hate all my kin."

"That ain't true," Caleb says. "In fact, I like your mother-in-law a whole lot better than I like mine."

Unexplained Attraction

Of someone who remains married to a jerk who's loud and obnoxious, you might say . . .

There's no accountin' for taste, as the ol' woman said when she kissed the cow.

Control Issues

To an overbearing and demanding friend who's wondering why his wife is threatening to leave him, you might say . . .

You're drivin' your mule too hard.

Intimate Bond

*Talking about a married couple
who think and act alike,
you might say . . .*

They're like two volumes
of the same book.

Bad Moments

*If you hit a few rough patches
in an otherwise good marriage,
you might say . . .*

Sometimes the better comes
after the worse.

Happy Marriage

If you're celebrating an anniversary that's reached double digits, you might want to tell your spouse . . .

Sure as water flows down hill, kissin' you is still a thrill.

Marital Acrimony

If you're fed up with your husband, you might say . . .

All men are idiots, and I married their king.

Mirror, Mirror
on the Wall . . .

Wynonna and her husband, Clayton, were getting ready for bed when she stood in front of their full-length mirror and examined her appearance for a spell. She shook her head and muttered, "I look in the mirror and see an old woman. My face is all wrinkled, my hair is gray, my shoulders are hunched over, I've got fat legs, and my arms are flabby."

She turned to her husband and pleaded, "Clayton, please tell me something positive to make me feel better about myself."

Clayton stared at her for a moment and then, in a thoughtful voice, said, "Pumpkin, there ain't nothin' wrong with your eyesight."

A Cure Worse Than the Disease

Pearl drove her ailing husband, Jethro, to the doctor's office in the next county. After the checkup, the doctor called Pearl into his office to speak to her alone.

"Your husband is suffering from a very severe stress disorder," the doctor explained. "If you don't follow my instructions to the letter, he won't live much longer. Every morning, fix him a big breakfast. Bake him a pie to serve at supper. Be pleasant at all times. Don't burden him with chores. Don't discuss your problems with him and, most important, don't nag him. It will only make his stress worse. If you can do this for the next year, I think your husband might regain his health completely."

On their way home, Jethro asked Pearl, "So what did the doctor say?"

Pearl shook her head and replied, "He said you was gonna die."

Reassuring Words

To your spouse who's worried about the future, you might say . . .

If the sky falls, we'll catch larks.

Assertive Woman

When referring to a marriage in which the wife rules the roost, you might say . . .

Now that there's a house run by a petticoat government.

Static Marriage

In describing a relationship in which neither partner has grown, you might say . . .

That marriage is like yesterday's corn bread—stale and dry.

Marital Diplomacy

In explaining why you cave in to your wife, you might say . . .

No use in me arguin' with her, 'cause it's like bringin' a knife to a gunfight.

Long Time Comin'

While enjoying an early morning breakfast in a small-town café, four elderly farmers jawed on subjects such as cattle, horses, the weather, and the good old days.

Eventually the conversation focused on their spouses. One of the farmers turned to his friend on the right and asked, "Buford, ain't you and the missus fixin' to celebrate your fiftieth weddin' anniversary soon?"

"Yup, we sure are," Buford replied.

"Are you gonna do something special to celebrate?" another farmer asked.

After swallowing a forkful of biscuits and gravy, Buford replied, "Well, for our fortieth anniversary, I took Bea to visit her sister over in Possum Hollow. Maybe for our fiftieth, I'll go down there and get her."

Anger Management

If your friend confides that he's angry at his wife, you might say . . .

Don't feel bad about thinkin' ill of her, 'cause she's probably thought worse 'bout you.

Tumultuous Twosome

About a couple who are always arguing, you might say . . .

There go blood and thunder.

Assertive Woman

A sign over the door of a quiet home might say . . .

My wife submits and I obey;
she always lets me have her way.

Marital Bribery

To an abusive husband who buys his wife nice things after each one of his transgressions, you might say . . .

Money will buy a fine dog, but
only kindness will make him
wag his tail.

It's All Relative

During a physical exam, the doctor told Orville, "It's odd for a strapping young lad like you to have such high blood pressure."

"It comes from my kin, Doc," said Orville.

"I've been taking care of your family for years, and there's never been a history of high blood pressure," the doctor countered.

"It don't come from my side of the family," Orville replied. "It comes from my wife's side."

"Oh, balderdash," the doctor said. "You can't get high blood pressure from your wife's side of the family."

Orville sighed and explained, "You haven't met my in-laws."

Critical Spouse

To your carping spouse,
you might say . . .

I feel like a banjo 'cause you're
always pickin' on me.

Happy Marriage

If you're celebrating an anniversary,
you might tell your spouse . . .

Sure as squirrels live in trees,
I'm for you and you're for me.

Housebroken

All the employees of the town's biggest and most successful cotton mill were married men.

When a strong-willed woman went to apply for a job there, she was turned down flat. Confronting the manager, she said, "Why do you hire only married men? Is it because you think women are weak, dumb, and cantankerous?"

"Not at all, Missy," the manager replied. "It's because married men are used to obeyin' orders, gettin' shoved around, keepin' their mouths shut, and not poutin' when they get yelled at."

The Last Word

Chester and his much younger friend Boyd were sitting out in front of the feed store playing checkers when Boyd asked, "How long have you been married?"

After some thought, Chester answered, "Pert near fifty years now, I reckon."

"Woo-ee!" Boyd exclaimed. "What's the secret?"

Chester leaned back in his chair and replied, "I always get in the last word whenever we kick up a ruckus."

"How do you manage that?" asked Boyd.

Answered Chester, "I tell her, 'Yes, Honey!'"

Marital Freedom

*As a reminder to your spouse
that each needs a bit of space,
you might say . . .*

A loose rein keeps the
marriage tight.

Aging Couple

*When talking to your spouse
about growing old together,
you might say . . .*

We're like a couple of prunes.
As time goes by, we're gettin'
wrinkled, but a whole lot sweeter.

Mad Money

After Russell carried his bride, Sara Jane, across the threshold of their first house, she placed a shoe box on a shelf in her closet and asked him never to touch it.

For fifty years Russell left the box alone. But one day, while he was searching for the deed to his pickup, he spotted the box. Caving in to temptation, he opened it. To his surprise, he found two doilies and $75,000 in cash. He put the box back in the closet.

Puzzled about what he had found, he confessed to Sara Jane that he had opened the box and begged her to explain the contents.

"Mama gave me that box the day you and I got hitched," Sara Jane explained. "She told me to make a doily for every time that I got mad at you." Russell was genuinely touched that in a half century, his wife had been mad at him only twice. "So where did the $75,000 come from?" he asked.

"Oh," replied Sara Jane, "that's the money I made from selling the rest of the doilies."

Foolish Argument

After a knock-down, drag-out, barn-burner of an argument, Bubba snarls at his wife, "Dadgummit, Betty Sue, I was a fool when I married you."

Betty Sue rubs her hands on her apron and replies, "I know, Bubba. But I was in love back then and didn't notice."

Marital Diplomacy

If you want to agree with your wife, you might say . . .

Whatever blows your dress up.

Reassuring Calm

If your spouse cheers you up after a tough day, you might tell your sweetie . . .

You give me comfort like sunshine after rain.

Bad Moments

As a reminder to your spouse not to focus too much on the unpleasant moments of an otherwise good marriage, you might say . . .

Count the orchard by the fruit
it bears and never by the
leaves that fall.

Happy Marriage

If you're celebrating an anniversary, you might tell your spouse . . .

Sure as young 'uns always ask
why, you are the apple of my eye.

Honest-to-Goodness Real Country Songs

You're the Hangnail in My Life,
and I Can't Bite You Off

You're the Reason Our
Kids Are Ugly

I Went Back to My Fourth Wife
for the Third Time and Gave
Her a Second Chance to Make
a First-Class Fool Out of Me

♥ ♥ ♥

If You Want Your Freedom PDQ,
Divorce Me COD

♥ ♥ ♥

This White Circle on My Finger
Means We're Through

♥ ♥ ♥

You Ain't Much Fun
Since I Quit Drinkin'

♥ ♥ ♥

You're a Hard Dog
to Keep Under the Porch

Don't Come Home A-Drinkin'
(With Lovin' on Your Mind)

If I Had to Do It All Over Again,
I'd Do It with You

Her Wedding Ring's a
One-Man Band

I Wish I Had Died at the Altar

I Wish I Had My First Wife Back

ROLLIN' IN THE HAY

(Look-Sees 'bout Sex)

Fish Tale

One Friday morning, Earl called home and told his wife, Leann, "Sugar Plum, the boss asked me to go on a fishin' trip with him and the other big shots for the weekend. Here's my chance to angle for that promotion you've been harpin' on me to get. Be an angel and pack up my clothes for the weekend and set out my rod and reel and tackle box. And don't forget to toss in my new blue pajamas. We're leavin' from the office so I'll swing by the house on the way out to pick up my things."

Leann's mind was swirling with suspicion but she did what she was told. A few hours later, Earl showed up at home just long enough to grab his things and give his wife a peck on the cheek. Then he flew out the door.

Sunday night, Earl returned bushed but otherwise fine. Leann welcomed him back and asked, "Did you catch many fish?"

"Yep," Earl replied. "We caught a mess of catfish and bluegill and a few crappies. By the way, how come you didn't pack my new blue pajamas like I asked you?"

"I did," said Leann, reaching for her rolling pin. "They were in your tackle box."

Cohabitation

- -

*If people wonder why you and
your partner don't get married,
you might say . . .*

No reason to buy the cow
when you can get the milk for free.

or

No reason to buy the pig
when you can get the sausage
for free.

Frustration

To a friend who complains that he isn't getting enough loving from his sweetheart, you might say . . .

If you ain't gettin' fed at home, then go out to eat.

Exhaustion

When you've had all the fun you can stand in bed, you might say . . .

I'm plumb tuckered out.

Some Things
You Never Forget

An elderly couple, Sadie Mae and Floyd, were sitting in their rockers on the porch, watching the beautiful sunset. Sadie turned to Floyd and said, "Lamb Chop, do you recollect when we first started sparkin' and you'd hold my hand?"

Floyd glanced over at his wife, grinned, and obligingly took her aged hand in his.

Batting her eyes, Sadie said, "Do you recollect how after we were engaged, you'd kiss me on the cheek?"

Floyd leaned over to his wife and gave her a lingering smooch.

Sadie smiled and said, "Do you recollect how, after we were first married, you'd nibble on my ear and then we'd go do the hoochie-coochie?"

Floyd sprang from his rocker and hobbled as fast as he could into the house.

Surprised, Sadie asked, "Lamb Chop, where are you goin'?"

Floyd yelled back, "To get my teeth!"

Beefcake

If your friends marvel at your lover's body, you might say . . .

He's as fit as a butcher's dog.

Cheating

When describing a tart who was caught cheating on her husband, you might say . . .

She was larkin' about and got her wings clipped.

Lover

*When asked to describe a
notorious lover, you might say . . .*

He's as wild as a peach
orchard hog.

Passion

*If you want to have another round in the
sack with your lover, you might say . . .*

Let's keep the pot a-boilin'.

Quandary

*To a friend who is wondering
if she should go home with the
cute guy she met at the party,
you might say . . .*

When you climb into the saddle,
you'd better be prepared to ride.

Gentleness

*In explaining to a friend why it's
important not to rush things in bed
with his girlfriend, you might say . . .*

The fastest way to move cattle
is slowly.

Fling

If you're talking to someone who's having an illicit affair, you might say . . .

What you do in the dark
will eventually come to light.

Passion

If you want to keep the bedsprings bouncing, you might say . . .

Let's keep whoopin' it up
'til the cows come home.

Skill

- -

*In describing an experienced
lover, you might say . . .*

He sure knows his onions.

Sexist

*If you're a sexist pig who thinks women
aren't worth dating unless they put out,
you might say . . .*

Color don't count if the horse
don't trot.

Ancestry

*Talking about someone who was born
out of wedlock and doesn't know her
father, you might say . . .*

She was born on the wrong side
of the blanket.

Seein' Is Believin'

Newlywed Ada Mae was getting plumb worn out by her husband, Farley's overactive sex drive. She finally confided to her minister who just happened to hold a psychology degree.

"I know your husband won't talk to me about this situation, but I have a plan," said the minister. He handed Ada Mae several numbered pages, each with a different ink blot on it. "Show these to your husband and write down what he says about each one," he instructed. "Then come back here and I'll try to figure out what the problem might be."

Later after dinner, Ada Mae brought out the ink blots. She held up the first one and asked Farley, "Dumplin', what do you see?"

He studied the ink blot for a moment and said, "That's a man and a woman havin' relations."

Showing him the next ink blot, she asked, "What's this a picture of?"

"A man and a woman havin' relations," Farley replied.

Ada Mae held up the third ink blot. "And what do you see here?"

"A man and a woman havin' relations."

Upset and frustrated, Ada Mae flung the rest of the ink blots onto the floor and declared, "You're just obsessed with sex!"

"Me?" Farley countered. "That ain't hardly fair. You're the one who keeps showin' me the dirty pictures!"

Waitin' for the Right Time

About midnight, a sheriff's deputy drives up to Lovers' Lane and recognizes a car belonging to his twenty-five-year-old cousin Hardy, the county's sleaziest womanizer. The deputy walks up to the car. To his surprise, he sees Hardy reading a book in the front seat and a sexy girl knitting in the back.

The deputy says, "Hardy, what are you two doin'?"

"Nothin' bad," Hardy replies. "I'm readin' and she's knittin'."

The cop turns to the girl and says, "You look mighty young. How old are you?"

She checks her watch and answers, "I'll be eighteen in 'bout five minutes."

Mistake

If your friend is moaning the morning after that she had sex with someone she wished she hadn't, you might say . . .

Well, the corn is off the cob.

Passion

If you hear a couple who are a little too loud in their lovemaking, you might say . . .

They're makin' more noise than a couple of jackasses in a tin barn.

Appeal

If you're ogling a sexy young thing, you might say . . .

I wouldn't kick her out of bed for eatin' soda crackers.

Exhaustion

When you've had all the fun you can stand in bed for the night, you might say . . .

Stick a fork in my buns ' cause I'm done.

A Question of Lust

After an all-nighter of passion, the young man whispers to his bride-to-be, "Sugar Lips, am I the first man to make love to you?"

"Of course you are, pumpkin," she says. Then she rolls her eyes and adds, "I don't know why you men always ask me the same ridiculous question."

Sex

As a way of suggesting the two
of you hop in the sack,
you might say . . .

Let's talk less and say more.

Rear

When talking about your sweetheart's
bare behind, you might say . . .

The first time I laid hands on
your Sunday face, I gave a prayer
of thanks.

Premarital Relations

*Talking about a couple who had a
child a few months after they married,
you might say . . .*

The young 'un didn't come early;
the weddin' came late.

Skill

*In giving advice to a friend
on making whoopee,
you might say . . .*

Fast is fine, but good is better.

Contentment

*If your lover asks how you feel
after a wild night of passion,
you might say . . .*

I'm slightly burned out,
but I'm still smokin'.

Secret

*As a warning to someone who is
trying to keep an illicit affair secret,
you might say . . .*

It'll all come out in the wash.

Saving Up for Marriage

For all his born days, seventy-year-old Otis had been a bachelor. But then he courted a twenty-five-year-old gold digger who agreed to marry him only after he told her he had been saving up for over fifty years.

After returning from their two-week honeymoon in the Bahamas, they attended a church social. With a big smile, a jaunty step and a twinkle in his eyes, Otis told his friends that getting married was the best thing he'd ever done. "I didn't see much of the sea or sun, if you get my drift," he boasted.

On the other side of the gathering, his young bride appeared dog tired and right haggard. "Lord have mercy!" exclaimed her friend. "You told me that after marryin' that old geezer you'd have it made in the shade. But you look like you've been run through the mill for a week and twice on Sunday. What happened?"

"Otis double-crossed me," the gold digger complained. "He told me he had saved up for over fifty years . . . and I thought he was talkin' about money!"

Passion

If you still have time for another roll in the hay before you have to go to work, you might say . . .

Don't stop kickin' 'til the clock stops tickin'.

Appeal

If you're ogling a hunk of burning love, you might say . . .

He can put his boots under my bed anytime.

Slut

- -

Talking about a woman who doesn't know who the father of her unborn baby is, you might say . . .

She ran through a patch of briars and don't know which one stuck her.

Cheating

- -

To someone who is fooling around on his wife, you might say . . .

You're gonna end up suppin' sorrow with a long spoon.

Passion

*Talking about the night you
and your sweetie were making love
with wild abandon, you might say . . .*

We were goin' at it like
killin' snakes.

Honest-to-Goodness Real Country Songs

I May Be Used
(But Baby, I Ain't Used Up)

Do You Love
as Good as You Look?

I'll Marry You Tomorrow
but Let's Honeymoon Tonight

She Offered Her Honor,
He Honored Her Offer, and
All Through the Night It
Was Honor and Offer

Get Your Biscuits in the Oven
and Your Buns in the Bed

Thanks to the Cathouse,
I'm in the Doghouse with You

You Done Me Wrong,
But at Least You Done Me

It Don't Feel Like Sinnin' to Me

Heaven's Just a Sin Away

Going to Hell in Your
Heavenly Arms

(I Can't Take Your Body)
If Your Heart's Not in It

♥ ♥ ♥

Now I Lay Me Down to Cheat

♥ ♥ ♥

If You Can't Be Good,
Be Bad with Me

♥ ♥ ♥

If You're Gonna Do Me Wrong,
Do It Right

♥ ♥ ♥

It Ain't Easy Being Easy

♥ ♥ ♥

Your Good Girl's Gonna Go Bad

Make Me Late for Work Today

I Never Went to Bed
with an Ugly Woman
(But I Sure Woke Up with a Few)

Think of Me
(When You're Under Him)

PARTIN' WAYS

(Digs an' Cuts 'bout Breakin' Up)

Cast Off

In describing how you got jilted by your girlfriend, you might say . . .

She flicked me off like a spent match.

Rejection

When talking about a woman who had turned down a beau's proposal and then booted him out of her life, you might say . . .

She sure gave him the mitten.

Put-Down

If you're splitting from your boyfriend after he did you wrong, you might say . . .

I wouldn't poke air holes in the top of a pickle jar if you were stuck inside.

Clash

In describing a rather loud breakup argument at a restaurant, you might say . . .

They went at it hammer and tongs.

Unsecured Loan

Loretta went to the bank to apply for a loan. "I want to borrow enough money to divorce my husband," she told the bank manager.

"Sorry, but we don't give loans for divorces" he said, "We make loans for appliances, automobiles, businesses, home improvements. . . ."

Loretta interrupted him and said, "Well, fine then. This certainly qualifies as a home improvement."

Shortcomings

If there are more drawbacks than benefits to sticking with a relationship, you might say . . .

I'd just as soon do without the eggs as to hear her cackle.

Cold Shoulder

In describing the silent treatment you received from your girlfriend when you broke up, you might say . . .

She wouldn't say pea turkey squat to me.

Breakup Advice

To a pal who's planning to break up with his girlfriend, you might say . . .

Speak your mind,
but ride a fast horse.

Divorce

If you're talking about a couple who got divorced, you might say . . .

She put him on the porch.

Put-Down

*If you're splitting from your
sweetheart after she did you wrong,
you might say . . .*

I wouldn't pee on you if you
were on fire.

Second Thoughts

*About someone you pursued and caught,
but then realized you really didn't want,
you might say . . .*

I guess my eyes were bigger
than my heart.

Pay Pal

"Mr. Bodine, I've reviewed the case very carefully," the divorce court judge says, "and I've decided to give your wife $275 a week."

"That'll work, Your Honor," Bodine concurs. "And every now and then I'll try to send her a few bucks myself."

Consequences

If your spouse left you because you were unfaithful, you might say . . .

I had her leavin' comin'.

Cast Off

Talking about a guy who was unceremoniously dumped by his girlfriend, you might say . . .

Oh, lordy, did he sit down on a bear trap.

Threat

To a friend who wants to threaten her boyfriend that she'll leave him even though she really wouldn't, you might say . . .

If you can't bite, don't growl.

Heartache

About someone who just got dumped and is taking it hard, you might say . . .

He'll be drinkin' his Christmas dinner.

Change

To a gal who split with her boyfriend after she failed to change his wild behavior, you might say . . .

You can't shoe a runnin' horse.

Put-Down

If you're breaking up because your partner was too cold and aloof, you might say . . .

You're as tender as a hangin' judge's heart.

Music to the Ears

Jesse called up his ex-wife, Trisha, and, while disguising his voice, asked, "Can I speak to Jesse, please?"

"Sorry, he don't live here no more," she answered. "We're divorced."

The next day, Jesse did the same thing and got the same answer. In fact, he called Trisha every day for a week until finally his ex-wife realized who was on the other end of the line. "Hey, you boil-brained weasel, we ain't married no more," Trisha railed. "When are you gonna get that through your fat head? We're divorced!"

"Oh, I know," Jesse responded calmly. "I just like hearing you say it."

Callousness

*About a girl who treated her
boyfriend badly before dumping him,
you might say . . .*

She walked across his heart
like it was Texas.

Glare

*If your girlfriend gave you the evil eye
after you suggested dating other people,
you might say . . .*

She looked mighty blue at me.

You Have the Right to Remain Silent

On the way home from the barn dance, Jake and his wife, Daisy, were cussing out each other in their pickup. The two were so all-fired up that it turned into a barn-burner — one that eventually turned their marriage into ashes.

Here's what happened: At the height of their donnybrook, Jake was pulled over by a policeman. The officer explained that he had stopped Jake because his taillight was burned out.

"I'm sorry, Officer," Jake said politely. "I didn't know it was out. I'll fix it right away."

But then Daisy piped up, "I knew this would happen. Jake, I told you two weeks ago to get that taillight fixed."

The officer frowned and asked for Jake's driver's license. After studying it, the cop said, "Sir, your license has expired."

Jake apologized profusely. "I didn't realize that, Officer. I promise to take care of it first thing in the morning."

Daisy let out a sarcastic laugh and said to Jake, "I told you a month ago that your license had expired and you wouldn't do anything about it."

By this time, Jake was getting a might ill with Daisy for contradicting him in front of the policeman. Losing his temper, Jake snapped, "Daisy, shut your cotton-pickin' trap!"

The officer leaned toward Daisy and asked, "Ma'am, does your husband always talk to you like that?"

Daisy replied smugly, "Only when he's drunk."

Consequences

About a guy whose sweet and loving wife finally divorced him because he kept straying from his marriage, you might say . . .

He just pissed in his whiskey.

Wrath

Talking about a wife who threw her husband out after he came home late and drunk for the umpteenth time, you might say . . .

She was as mad as a calf with a barbwire tail.

Heartache

*To a friend who's been pining
away for days over a lost love,
you might say . . .*

Don't just lay there and bleed.

Breakup Advice

*To a friend who wants to dump her
lover because she's got her eyes on
another guy, you might say . . .*

Don't throw away the old bucket
'til you know whether the new one
holds water.

No Return Policy

At the square dance, Mary Lou goes over to Lacy Jane and whispers, "I hear tell you broke off your engagement to Calvin. What happened?"

"It's just that my feelin's toward him ain't the same anymore," Lacy Jane replies.

"Are you fixin' to give back the ring?"

"Heavens, no!" says Lacy Jane. "My feelin's toward the ring haven't changed one iota."

Vexation

*In explaining why you split from your
girlfriend, you might say . . .*

She was so exasperatin'
she could make a preacher cuss.

Cheater

*If you caught your lover cheating
on you, you might say . . .*

You must have been hidin' behind
the door when they were passin'
out morals.

Abuser

*If you're leaving your abusive lover,
you might say . . .*

I'd rather jump barefoot off a
six-foot stepladder into a
five-gallon bucket full of
porcupines than spend another
night with you.

Spendthrift

*If you're splitting up with your
boyfriend because he's so cheap,
you might say . . .*

You're as tight as a hawk's butt
in a nosedive.

Rage

*In describing to your friends
later how angry you were at him when
he broke up with you, you might say . . .*

I sure gave 'em down the country!

Heartbreak

*If you're still sad over your recent
breakup, you might say . . .*

I've had the blue devils all week.

A Failure to Communicate

Earnest the farmer walked into the country lawyer's office and announced, "I want to get one of them divorces."

The lawyer said, "Do you have any grounds?"

"Yep, I got about one hundred forty acres."

The lawyer chuckled and said, "You don't understand. Do you have a case?"

"No, I ain't got no Case. I got a John Deere."

Feeling a touch of frustration, the lawyer asked, "I mean do you have a grudge?"

"Yep, I got a grudge. That's where I park my Case."

The lawyer tried to remain calm, but it wasn't easy. He decided to try a different line of questioning. "Do you have a suit?"

"Yep. I wear it to church on Sundays."

The lawyer took a deep breath and, holding his irritation in check, asked, "Well, does your wife beat you up?"

"Nope. We both get up the same time."

Finally, in exasperation, the lawyer bellowed, "Why in God's green earth do you want a divorce?"

Earnest replied, "I can't never have a meanin'ful conversation with her."

Vexation

*If you can't convince your sweetheart
that he's making a huge mistake in
suggesting you date other people,
you might say . . .*

If you can't change your mind,
are you sure you have one?

Cheater

*To a guy who has been unfaithful
to you, you might say . . .*

You can cheat a fish out
of its scales.

Jerk

*If you're breaking up with a guy
who pretends to be a gentleman but is
really an arrogant, egotistical cad,
you might say . . .*

You're nothin' but a barber's clerk.

Heartache

*Seeing the sad look on a
friend who got dumped,
you might say . . .*

You have a face as long as
a Missouri mule.

Divorce Advice

*If your divorced friend asks
what he should do with his old
wedding ring, you might say . . .*

Ain't no need for pockets
on a dead man's coat.

Rage

*To the guy who angered you so much
that you dumped him on
the spot, you might say . . .*

Go boil your shirt!

Incompatibility

In explaining why you're splitting with your lover because neither of you gets along anymore, you might say . . .

The two of us just can't seem to gee-haw.

Put-Down

To your ex-lover, you might say . . .

You are the raspberry seed between my teeth.

Oppression

If you're breaking up because your partner has been smothering you to death, you might say . . .

Love can't grow in the shade.

Liar

If you're splitting up with someone who lies all the time, you might say . . .

I'm ditchin' your sorry behind 'cause you're too tight with the truth.

For Love
or Money

Dear Sweet Pea,

I've been so down in the mouth ever since I broke off our engagement. I was dead wrong. I must have been touched in the head. Won't you please offer forgiveness and come back to me? You hold a cherished place in my heart that no other woman will ever touch. We were made for each other like biscuits and gravy. I love you so.

Yours forever and ever,
Buck

P.S. Congratulations on winning the million-dollar lottery!

Nit-Picker

*To the woman you're dumping because
you can't take her incessant carping
any longer, you might say . . .*

You'd complain if your ice cream
were cold and hell weren't
hot enough.

Cheater

*If you're splitting from your man
because he cheated on you,
you might say . . .*

You hurt the love right out of me.

Heartache

*If your loved one is thinking
of breaking up with you,
you might say . . .*

Good-bye ain't painful unless you
ain't plannin' on sayin' hello again.

Fury

*In describing how loud the girl was
swearing at her boyfriend during their
breakup, you might say . . .*

Oh, was she airin' out her lungs.

Tenacity

*If you're not ready to quit
a relationship even though
your partner already has,
you might say . . .*

Don't forget me 'cause if you do,
I ain't leavin'.

Cheater

*To the cad you're breaking up with
because he went out with your
best friend, you might say . . .*

You're so low you could walk
under a snake without bendin'
your knees.

Critic

- -

*To the lover you're dumping because
he's always criticizing you,
you might say . . .*

Love don't keep no lists of wrongs.

Heartache

- -

*If you got your heart broken when you
got jilted, you might say . . .*

She struck a match to the
book of love.

Divorce Advice

In offering support to a friend who's wondering if she should go through with a divorce, you might say . . .

Go ahead and choke the horn and claw the leather.

Honest-to-Goodness
Real Country Songs

You Changed Your Name from
Brown to Jones, and Mine from
Brown to Blue

How Can I Miss You
If You Won't Go Away?

She Got the Gold Mine
and I Got the Shaft

My Wife Ran Off with My Best
Friend, and I Sure Do Miss Him

♥ ♥ ♥

Thank God and Greyhound
She's Gone

♥ ♥ ♥

If You Don't Leave Me Alone
(I'll Find Someone Else Who Will)

♥ ♥ ♥

I Was Looking Back to See if
You Were Looking Back to See if
I Was Looking Back to See if You
Were Looking Back at Me

♥ ♥ ♥

Get Your Tongue Outta My
Mouth 'Cause I'm Kissin' You
Good-bye

♥ ♥ ♥

All My Exes Live in Texas

If the Phone Don't Ring, It's Me

If You Can't Live Without Me,
Why Aren't You Dead?

She Made Toothpicks from
the Timber of My Heart

If Fingerprints Showed Up
on Skin, Wonder Whose I'd
Find on You

I Keep Forgettin' I Forgot
About You

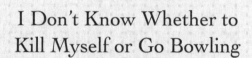

I Don't Know Whether to
Kill Myself or Go Bowling

♥ ♥ ♥

I'm So Miserable Without You
(It's Almost Like You're Here)

♥ ♥ ♥

Billy Broke My Heart at
Walgreens and I Cried All the Way
to Sears

♥ ♥ ♥

I Bought the Shoes That Just
Walked Out on Me

♥ ♥ ♥

If Drinkin' Don't Kill Me,
Her Memory Will

♥ ♥ ♥

All I Want from You (Is Away)

♥ ♥ ♥

She's Actin' Single
(I'm Drinkin' Doubles)

♥ ♥ ♥

Here's a Quarter
(Call Someone Who Cares)

♥ ♥ ♥

Flushed You from the
Toilets of My Heart

♥ ♥ ♥

My Lips Want to Stay
(But My Heart Wants to Go)

♥ ♥ ♥

Which Way Do I Go
(Now That I'm Gone)?

♥ ♥ ♥

Drinking to Forget What
I'm Drinking to Forget

♥ ♥ ♥

I Can't Get Over You 'til
You Get Out from Under Him

♥ ♥ ♥

I Miss You Already
(And You're Not Even Gone)

♥ ♥ ♥

I Need Somebody Bad Tonight
('Cause I Just Lost Somebody
Good)

I've Got Tears in My Ears from
Lyin' on My Back in Bed and
Cryin' on My Pillow Over You

She Got the Green
and I Got the Blues

When You Leave, Walk Out
Backwards So I'll Think
You're Walking In

You're the Reason
I'm Not Over You

If You Leave Me,
Can I Come Too?

GOSPEL TRUTHS

('Bout Men an' Women,
Love an' Marriage)

Marriage

If you don't have a sense of humor
in your marriage, you probably
don't have no sense at all.

Work at havin' a good marriage.
That way, when you get older and
look back at your lives together,
you'll enjoy it a second time.

Don't marry the man you can
live with. Marry the man you
can't live without.

Some women get excited
about nothin' . . . and then
marry him.

The best thing to hold on to in life
is each other.

A house is built with boards
and beams . . . A home is built with
love and dreams

Happiness is home brewed.

Have love in your heart and
peace in your home.

A happy home is the father's
kingdom, the mother's world, and
the child's paradise.

The calmest husbands
make the stormiest wives.

Never marry for money.
You can borrow it cheaper.

More things belong to marriage
than four bare legs in a bed.

A deaf husband and a blind wife
are always a happy couple.

Marriage is a shortcut to a
long life.

A happy home is but an
early heaven.

No matter what, no matter where,
it's always home if love is there.

Love ain't a matter of countin'
the years. What matters is makin'
he years count.

If love is blind, marriage is a
real eye-opener.

Any married man should forget
his mistakes 'cause there ain't
no use in two people recollectin'
the same things.

♥ ♥ ♥

Life's a voyage that's
homeward bound.

♥ ♥ ♥

A woman marries a man expectin'
he'll change, but he don't. A man
marries a woman expectin' she
won't change, but she does.

There are two times when a man
don't understand a woman —
before marriage and after.

If love is one long sweet dream,
marriage is the rooster's crow.

Memories are stitched with love.

Have a heart that never hardens,
a temper that never tires,
and a touch that never hurts.

Love and marriage go together
like grits and gravy.

Dating

When it comes to datin', there are
more horses' asses than horses.

Women

Women come and go,
but your tools last forever.

Men

Men are like the weather.
Nothin' can be done to change 'em.

Personal Experience

When Wanda Sue stood in the checkout line at the local Piggly Wiggly, she showed off her engagement ring to the cashier.

Zack, a grizzled good ol' boy with a six-pack under each arm, was next in line. He congratulated Wanda Sue and then offered her an observation about marriage. "The first ten years are the hardest," he said.

"How long have you been married?" Wanda Sue asked.

Replied Zack, "Ten years."

Anger

An angry bull is less dangerous
than an angry woman.

Spooning

A man chases a woman
until she catches him.

Sucker

Don't kiss a fool or let a kiss
fool you.

Men

Men are like barbwire—
they have their bad points.

Quarrel

There are two beliefs about arguin' with women, and neither one of 'em works.

Drinking

A smile from a good woman is worth more than a dozen from a bartender.

Flour Girl

Bo and his wife, Roxanne, were attending a church gathering, listening intently to the minister talk about the need for communication in marriage.

"It is essential that husbands and wives know each other's likes and dislikes," the minister said. Turning to Bo, he asked, "Can you name your wife's favorite flower?"

Bo felt pretty confident in his answer. He leaned over, patted his wife's hand and said, "It's Pillsbury, ain't it, angel?"

Fool

Only a fool argues with a skunk,
a mule, or a wife who can cook.

Men

Men are like pears.
The older they are, the softer
they get.

Priorities

- -

The most important things a man
can get in this world are somethin'
to eat, somethin' to drink, and
someone to love.

Deadly Demands

Dewey was a mild-mannered man
who was tired of being bossed
around by his wife, Marvella, so he
went to his preacher to complain.
The preacher said Dewey needed to
build up his self-esteem and gave him
a lecture on assertiveness. "You must
tell her exactly what it is you want
from her," the preacher told him.

After the session, Dewey was all
fired up and stormed into the house.
Pointing a finger in Marvella's face,
he thundered, "From now on, I
am the man of this house, and my
word is law! Tonight you will fix
me country-fried steak with cherry
cobbler. When I'm finished eatin',

you're gonna draw me a nice, relaxin' bath. And when I'm finished with that, guess who's gonna dress me and comb my hair?"

With a stone face, Marvella replied, "The funeral director."

Precise Advice

Old Man Haywood was having a heart-to-heart with Kenny, a strapping young lad who was on the lookout for the right girl to marry.

"Son, take it from me," said Haywood. "There are four things every man should know when huntin' for a wife. One, find a woman who's good at household chores and can cook up a storm. Two, find a woman who loves to go dancin' and can hold her liquor. Three, find a woman who'll make whoopee with you anytime, anywhere."

"What's the fourth thing?" asked Kenny.

Replied Haywood, "It is very important that these three women never meet."

Understanding

To be happy with a man,
you need to understand him a lot
and love him a little. To be happy
with a woman, you need to love
her a lot and not understand her
at all.

Quarrel

A woman has the last word in any
argument. Anythin' a man says
after that is the beginnin' of
a new argument.

Men

Women don't make fools of men
'cause most men can do it
themselves.

Honesty

It's better to be hated for who you
are than loved for who you ain't.

Love

True love is when you're still dancin' long after the music stopped.

Fallin' in love ain't so hard. It's like strollin' through a pasture — sooner or later you're gonna step in it.

Love puts the joy in bein' together and the sadness in bein' apart.

Love is like wildflowers —
it blooms in the most
unlikely places.

Love is the reason two people sit
in the middle of the bench when
there's room on both ends.

Life with your sweetie don't have
to be perfect to be wonderful.

Go after love as if it's somethin'
that's got to be roped in a hurry
before it gets away.

421

Makin' it in love is kind of like
bustin' broncos. You're gonna get
thrown a lot. The secret is to keep
gettin' back on.

Love ain't love 'til you give it away.

A true love stays when the rest of
the world walks out.

Seeds of love always bloom
with joy.

It's easy to fall in love.
The hard part is findin' someone
to catch you.

Love is like checkers,
except both sides win.

A heart that loves is always young.

Live by the sun, love by the moon.

Love is like kudzu — it spreads.

To feel rich, count all the things
you and your sweetheart have
that money can't buy.

To love and be loved is to feel the
sun from both sides.